Defending
the
Undefendable

Defending
the
Undefendable

The Pimp, Prostitute, Scab, Slumlord, Libeler,
Moneylender, and Other Scapegoats in the
Rogue's Gallery of American Society

Walter Block

MISES
INSTITUTE
Auburn, Alabama

Published 2018 by the Ludwig von Mises Institute
This work is licensed under a Creative Commons
Attribution-NonCommercial-NoDerivs 4.0 International
License. http:/creativecommons.org/licenses/by-nc-nd/4.0

Ludwig von Mises Institute
518 West Magnolia Avenue
Auburn, Alabama 36832
Mises.org.

ISBN: 978-1-933550-17-6

This book is dedicated to those who have taught me political economy and inspired me with a passion for justice:

Nathaniel Branden
Walter E. Grinder
Henry Hazlitt
Benjamin Klein
Ayn Rand
Jerry Woloz

and especially Murray N. Rothbard

CONTENTS

FOREWORD

For many years, free-market economists have shown how market activities benefit the often heedless public. Ever since the days of Adam Smith, they have shown how producers and businessmen, generally motivated solely by personal gain, unwittingly confer enormous benefits on the general public. By seeking to maximize their profits and minimize losses, for example, businessmen are driven to satisfy the most urgent demands of the consumers in the most efficient way. Economists have long shown these truths *in the abstract*; and in recent years they have added to our knowledge by illustrating in case after case, in the concrete, the superiority and efficiency of private operation. But the inquiries of economists have been confined, with sober pedantry, to the "respectable" industries: to such activities as agriculture, natural gas, housing, airways, and so forth. Until this book, no economist has had the courage of Professor Walter Block in tackling head-on the moral and economic status of the dozens of reviled, scorned, and grievously misunderstood professions and occupations in our society: those whom he rightly calls the "economic scapegoats." Fearlessly, and with logic and trenchant wit, Professor Block rehabilitates and demonstrates the considerable economic merits of such scapegoat occupations as the pimp, the blackmailer, and the slumlord. In this way, in addition to redeeming the stature of these much reviled occupations, *Defending the Undefendable* performs the service of highlighting, in the fullest and starkest terms, the essential nature of the productive services performed by all people in the free market. By taking the most extreme examples and showing how the Smithian principles work even in these cases, the book does far more to demonstrate the workability and morality of the free market than a dozen sober tomes on more respectable industries and activities. By testing and proving the extreme cases, he all the more illustrates and vindicates the theory.

These case studies also have considerable shock value. By relentlessly taking up one "extreme" case after another that is generally guaranteed to shock the sensibilities of the reader, Professor Block forces the reader to think, to rethink his initial knee-jerk emotional responses, and to gain a new and far sounder appreciation of economic theory and of the virtues and operations of the free-market economy. Even many readers who now *think* they believe in a free market must now be prepared to grasp fully the logical implications of a belief in a free economy. This book will be an exciting and shocking adventure for most readers, even for those who believe that they are already converted to the merits of the free-market economy.

All right, some readers might concede, we grant that these people *are* performing valuable economic services. But why, for heaven's sake, call them "heroes"? Why is the pimp or the medical quack any more "heroic," and therefore in a sense more moral, than other, more respectable producers: the grocers, clothiers, steel manufacturers, etc.? The explanation is precisely wrapped up in the extreme lack of respectability of Professor Block's scapegoats. For the grocer, the steel producer, and the others are generally allowed to go about their business unmolested, and indeed earn respect and prestige from the fellow members of the community. Not so these scapegoats; for not only are their economic services unrecognized, but they face the universal bile, scorn, and wrath of virtually every member of society, plus the additional restrictions and prohibitions that governments have almost universally placed upon their activities. Scorned and condemned unmercifully by society and state alike, social outcasts and state-proclaimed outlaws, Professor

Block's collection of scapegoats go about their business nevertheless; heroically proceeding to confer their economic services in the teeth of universal scorn and outlawry. They are heroes indeed, made so by their unjust treatment at the hands of society and of the state apparatus.

Heroes yes, but not necessarily *saints*. When the author confers the moral stature of hero on the scab, the usurer, the pimp, and so on, he does not mean to imply that these activities are intrinsically more moral than any other. In a free market, and in a society that treats the usurer, slumlord, and sweat shop employer in precisely the same just way as it treats other occupations, they would no longer be heroes, and they would certainly be no more moral than anyone else. Their heroic status, for Professor Block, is solely a function of the unjust restrictions that other men have been placing upon them. It is the happy paradox of this book that if its implicit advice is followed, and the men and women described in these pages are no longer treated to scorn and legal coercion, then and only then will they no longer be heroes. If you don't like the idea of a usurer or a slumlord being a hero, then the *only* way to deprive him of this stature is to remove the shackles that misguided people have placed upon him.

Murray N. Rothbard

COMMENTARY

Looking through *Defending the Undefendable* made me feel that I was once more exposed to the shock therapy by which, more than fifty years ago, the late Ludwig von Mises converted me to a consistent free market position. Even now I am occasionally at first incredulous and feel that "this is going too far," but usually find in the end that you are right. Some may find it too strong a medicine, but it will still do them good even if they hate it. A real understanding of economics demands that one disabuses oneself of many dear prejudices and illusions. Popular fallacies in economics frequently express themselves in unfounded prejudices against other occupations, and in showing the falsity of these stereotypes you are doing a real service, although you will not make yourself more popular with the majority.

F.A. von Hayek, Nobel Laureate
Institut for Nationalökonomie
Universität Salzburg

INTRODUCTION

The people presented in this book are generally considered villainous, and the functions they perform, harmful. Sometimes society itself is damned because it spawns such reprehensible characters. However, the thrust of this book will concentrate on the following propositions:

1. they are guilty of no wrongdoing of a violent nature;
2. in virtually every case, they actually benefit society;
3. if we prohibit their activities, we do so at our own loss.

The impetus for this book is Libertarianism. The basic premise of this philosophy is that *it is illegitimate to engage in aggression against nonaggressors*. What is meant by aggression is not assertiveness, argumentativeness, competitiveness, adventurousness, quarrelsomeness, or antagonism. What is meant by aggression is the use of violence, such as that which takes place in murder, rape, robbery, or kidnapping. Libertarianism does not imply pacifism; it does not forbid the use of violence in defense or even in retaliation against violence. Libertarian philosophy condemns only the *initiation of violence*—the use of violence against a nonviolent person or his property.

There is nothing untoward or controversial about such a view. Most people would give it their wholehearted support. Indeed, this sentiment is part and parcel of our Western civilization, enshrined in the law, in our Constitution, and in the natural law.

The uniqueness of Libertarianism is found not in the statement of its basic principle but in the rigorously consistent, even maniacal manner with which the principle is applied. For example, most people do not see any contradiction between this principle and our system of taxation. Libertarians do.

Taxation is contrary to the basic principle because it involves aggression against nonaggressive citizens who refuse to pay. It makes not the slightest difference that the government offers goods and services in return for the tax money. What is important is that the so-called "trade" (tax money for government services) is *coerced*. The individual is not free to reject the offer. Nor does the fact that a majority of the citizens support this coercive taxation make any difference. The initiation of aggression, even when endorsed by the majority, is not legitimate. Libertarianism condemns it in this area as it condemns it wherever it occurs.

Another difference between the beliefs of Libertarians and the beliefs of other members of society is the obverse of the view that initiatory violence is evil. Libertarians maintain that as far as political theory is concerned, anything which does *not* involve the initiation of violence is not evil and that as far as political theory is concerned, anything which does not involve the initiation of violence is not a punishable evil and should not be outlawed. And this is the basis for the first part of my argument. The so-called "villains" are not villains at all, in this sense, because *they do not initiate violence against nonaggressors*.

Once it is realized that no one in this seeming rogue's gallery is guilty of any coercive wrongdoing, it is not difficult to appreciate the second point: *virtually all of the people with whom we are concerned are responsible for benefiting the rest of society.* The people we are considering are not aggressors. They do not force themselves on anyone. If the other members of the community have any dealings with them, these dealings are voluntary. People engage in voluntary transactions because they feel that some benefit can be derived. Since people voluntarily trade with our "villains," they must get from them something they desire. The "villains" *must* be providing a benefit.

The third premise follows ineluctably from the second. Given that voluntary trade (the only avenue of interaction open to those who, like the scapegoats, have eschewed violence) must always benefit all parties, it follows that the prohibition of voluntary trade must *harm* all parties. In fact, my point is even stronger. I will argue that prohibiting the activities of the people we are considering harms not only the potential parties to the trade, but it can seriously harm third parties. One blatant example is the prohibition of the activities of the heroin seller. In addition to harming the seller and the customer, the prohibition of the sale of heroin is responsible for a high proportion of the crime committed in our society, for police graft, and in many areas, for the general breakdown of law and order.

The chief point I wish to make in this introduction—the core of my position—is that there is a crucial difference between the initiation of aggression and all other acts which, while they may displease us, do not involve such aggression. It is *only* the act of aggressive violence that violates man's rights. Refraining from aggressive violence must be considered a fundamental law of society. The people dealt with in this book, though reviled by the media and condemned out of hand by almost everyone, do not violate anyone's rights, so they should not be subjected to judicial sanctions. It is my belief that they are scapegoats—they are visible, they are available to attack, but they must be defended, if justice is to prevail.

This book is a defense of the marketplace. It singles out for special praise those participants in the free enterprise system who are the most reviled by its critics. It does so because if the price system can be shown to be mutually beneficial and productive in these extreme examples, then the case for markets in general is strengthened even the more.

However, it is important to counteract one possible misinterpretation. This book does *not* claim that the marketplace is a moral economic institution. True, the profit and loss business system has brought mankind a plethora of consumer goods and services unknown in the entire history of the world. These benefits are the envy of all peoples not fortunate enough to live under its banner. Given the tastes, desires, preferences of the ultimate consumer, the market is the best means known to man for providing for his satisfaction.

But the marketplace also produces goods and services—such as gambling, prostitution, pornography, drugs (heroin, cocaine, etc.), alcohol, cigarettes, swinger's clubs, suicide abettment—whose moral status is, to say the least, highly questionable and in many cases highly immoral. The free enterprise system, thus, cannot be considered a moral one. Rather, as a means of consumer satisfaction, it can only be as moral as are the goals of the market participants themselves. Since these vary widely, all the way from the completely depraved and immoral to the entirely legitimate, the market must be seen as amoral—neither moral nor immoral.

The market in other words is like fire, or a gun, or a knife, or a typewriter: a splendidly efficient means toward both good and bad ends. Through free enterprise we are capable of achieving virtuous actions, but also their very opposite as well.

How, then, can we defend the immoral activities of some market actors? This stems from the philosophy of libertarianism, which is limited to analyzing one single problem. It asks, under what conditions is violence justified? And it answers, violence is justified only for purposes of defense, or in response to prior aggression, or in retaliation against it. This means, among other things, that government is not justified in fining, punishing, incarcerating, imposing death penalties on people who act in an immoral manner—as long as they refrain from threatening or initiating physical violence on the persons or property of others. Libertarianism, then, is not a philosophy of life. It does not presume to indicate how mankind may best live. It does not set out the boundaries between the good and the bad, between the moral and the immoral, between propriety and impropriety.

The defense of such as the prostitute, pornographer, etc., is thus a very limited one. It consists solely of the claim that they do not initiate physical violence against nonaggressors. Hence, according to libertarian principles, none should be visited upon them. This means only that these activities should not be punished by jail sentences or other forms of violence. It decidedly does *not* mean that these activities are moral, proper, or good.

Walter Block

I. SEXUAL

1

THE PROSTITUTE

Subject to ceaseless harassment by blue laws, church groups, chambers of commerce, etc., prostitutes nevertheless continue to trade with the public. The value of their service is proven by the fact that people continue to seek them out, despite legal and civic opposition.

A prostitute may be defined as one who engages in the voluntary trade of sexual services for a fee. The essential part of the definition, however, is "voluntary trade." A magazine cover by Norman Rockwell some time ago illustrated the essence of prostitution, if not the specifics. It portrayed a milkman and a pieman standing near their trucks, each busily eating a pie and drinking milk. Both obviously pleased with their "voluntary trade."

Those lacking sufficient imagination will see no connection between the prostitute entertaining her customer and the aforementioned milk and pie episode. But in both cases, two people have come together on a voluntary basis, in an attempt to mutually gain satisfaction. In neither case is force or fraud applied. Of course, the customer of the prostitute may later decide that the services he received were not worth the money he paid. The prostitute may feel that the money she was paid did not fully compensate her for the services she provided. Similar dissatisfactions could also occur in the milk-pie trade. The milk could have been sour or the pie underbaked. But both regrets would be *after the fact* and would not alter the description of these trades as "voluntary." If all the participants were not willing, the trades would not have taken place.

There are those, women's liberationists among them, who lament the plight of the poor downtrodden prostitute, and who think of her life as demeaning and exploitative. But the prostitute does not look upon the sale of sex as demeaning. After considering the good features (short hours, high remuneration), with the drawbacks (harassment by the police, enforced commissions to her pimp, uninspiring working conditions), the prostitute obviously prefers her work, otherwise she would not continue it.

There are of course many negative aspects experienced by prostitutes which belie the "happy hooker" image. There are prostitutes who are drug addicts, prostitutes who are beaten by pimps, and prostitutes who are held in brothels against their will. But these sordid aspects have little to do with the intrinsic career of prostitution. There are nurses and doctors who are kidnapped and forced to perform for fugitives from justice; there are carpenters who are drug addicts; there are bookkeepers who are beaten by muggers. We would hardly conclude that any of these professions or vocations are suspect, demeaning, or exploitative. The life of the prostitute is as good or as bad as she wishes it to be. She enters it voluntarily, *qua* prostitute, and is free to leave at any time.

Why then the harassment and prohibitions against prostitution? The momentum does not come from the customer; he is a willing participant. If the customer decides that patronization of a prostitute is not to his advantage, he can stop. Nor does the move toward prohibition of prostitution come from the prostitutes themselves. They have volunteered for their tasks, and can almost always quit if they change their minds about the relative benefits.

The impetus for the prohibition of prostitution is initiated by "third parties" not directly involved in the trades. Their reasons vary from group to group, from area to area, and from year to year. What they have in common is the fact that they are outside parties. They have neither stake nor standing in the matter, and should be ignored. To allow them to decide this matter is as absurd as allowing an outsider to decide about the trade between the milkman and the pieman.

Why then are the two cases treated differently? Imagine a league called the "decent eaters," organized to espouse the doctrine that eating pie together with milk is evil. Even if it could be demonstrated that the league against pie-and-milk and the league against prostitution had identical intellectual merit— namely, none—the reaction to the two would still be different. The attempt to prohibit pie and milk would evoke only laughter but there would be a more tolerant attitude toward the attempt to prohibit prostitution. There is something in operation which staunchly resists an intellectual penetration of the prostitution question. Why has prostitution not been legalized? Though the arguments against this legalization are without merit, they have never been clearly assailed by the intellectual community as specious.

The difference between sexual trades such as the ones that take place in prostitution, and other trades, such as the pie-milk trade, seems to be based on, or at least connected to, the shame we feel, or are made to feel, at the prospect of having to *buy* sex." One is hardly "really a man," nor in any way to be confused with an attractive woman, if one pays for sex.

The following well-known joke illustrates this point. A good looking man asks an attractive and "virtuous" woman if she will go to bed with him for $100,000.00. She is appalled by the offer. However, after some reflection she concludes that as evil as prostitution is, she could use the proceeds of the offer for charity and good works. The man seems charming, not at all dangerous or repugnant. She shyly says, "Yes." The man then asks: "How about for $20.00?" The woman indignantly replies, "How dare you, what kind of woman do you think I am!" as she slaps his face. "Well we've already established what kind of woman you are. Now, we're trying to establish the price," he replies. The degree to which the man's reply strikes a telling blow against the woman is a small measure of the scorn heaped upon individuals involved in this kind of endeavor.

There are two approaches which might combat the attitude that paying for sex is degrading. There is the frontal attack which simply denies that it is a wrong to pay for sex. This, however, would hardly convince those who think of prostitution as an evil. The other possibility would be to show that we are *always* paying for sex—all of us, all the time—and, therefore, we should not cavil at the arrangements between a professional prostitute and a customer.

In what sense can it be said that we all engage in trade and payments when we engage in sexual activity? At the very least, we have to offer *something* to our prospective partners before they will consent to have sex with us. With explicit prostitution, the offer is in terms of cash. In other cases, the trade is not so obvious. Many dating patterns clearly conform to the prostitutional model. The male is expected to pay for the movies, dinners, flowers, etc., and the female is expected to reciprocate with sexual services. The marriages in which the husband provides the financial elements, and the wife the sexual and housekeeping functions, also conforms clearly enough to the model.

In fact, all voluntary human relationships, from love relationships to intellectual relationships, are trades. In the case of romantic love and marriage, the trade is in terms of affection, consideration, kindness, etc. The trade may be a happy one, and the partners may find joy in the giving. But it is still a trade. It is clear that unless affection, kindness, etc., or *something* is given, it will not be reciprocated. In the same way, if two "nonmercenary" poets did not "get anything" from each other, their relationship too would terminate.

If there are trades, there are also payments. Where there are payments for relationships which include sexual congress such as marriage and in some dating patterns—there is prostitution—according to the definition of that term. Several social commentators have correctly likened marriage to prostitution. But all relationships where trade takes place, those which include sex as well as those which do not, are a form of prostitution. Instead of condemning all such relationships because of their similarity to prostitution, prostitution should be viewed as just one kind of interaction in which all human beings participate. Objections should not be raised to any of them—not to marriage, not to friendship, not to prostitution.

2

THE PIMP

From time immemorial, pimps have been treated as parasites who prey on prostitutes. But in a fair assessment, an examination of the true function of the pimp must be made.

An initial point requiring clarification is the claim that pimps use coercion and threats of violence to gather and keep prostitutes on their payrolls. Some pimps do, but does this fact justify condemning the profession itself? Is there *any* profession that does not have a single practitioner who is not guilty of foul play? There are bricklayers, plumbers, musicians, priests, doctors, and lawyers who have violated the rights of their fellow creatures. But these professions are not *qua* professions to be condemned in their entirety.

And so it should be with the profession of pimping. The actions of any one, or even of all pimps together, cannot legitimately be used to condemn the profession *qua* profession, *unless the action is a necessary part of the profession*. Now the profession of kidnapping small children for ransom is an evil profession, *qua profession*. Even though some kidnappers may perform good deeds, such as contributing a part of the ransom to charity, or even if all of them do so, the profession does not thereby become less of an abomination, because the action which defines it is

9

*"Look, I'm her father, I'm only interested in her wel-
fare—but she won't listen to me! Please talk to her—
tell her to come home with me to Akron. She'll listen to
you, you're her pimp."*

evil. If the action which defines the profession of pimping were
evil, then it should be condemned also. In order to evaluate
pimping, any extraneous evil acts which may be committed by
some pimps must be ignored as having little to do with the profession as such.

The function of the pimp *qua* pimp is that of a broker. In the
same way as do brokers of real estate, insurance, stock market

shares, investments, commodity futures, etc., the pimp serves the function of bringing together two parties to a transaction at less cost than it would take to bring them together without his good offices. Each party to a transaction served by a broker gains from the brokerage, otherwise they would not patronize him. And so it is in the case of the pimp. The customer is spared useless or wasteful waiting and searching time. It is easier to phone a pimp for an assignation with a prostitute than to spend time and effort searching one out. The customer also has the security of knowing that the prostitute comes recommended.

The prostitute benefits too. She gains the time that would otherwise be spent in searching for the customer. She is also protected by the pimp—from undesirable customers, and from policemen, part of whose profession, *qua* profession, is to prevent prostitutes from engaging in voluntary trade with consenting adults. Assignations arranged by the pimp afford the prostitute additional physical security over street walking or bar hopping.

The prostitute is no more exploited by the pimp than is the manufacturer exploited by the salesman who drums up business for him, or the actress who pays an agent a percentage of her earnings to find new roles for her. In these examples the employer, by means of the employee's services, earns more than the cost of hiring the employee. If this were not so, the employer-employee relationship would not take place. The relationship of the prostitute to the pimp (employer to employee), contains the same mutual advantages.

The professional pimp performs the necessary function of brokering. In this performance he is if anything more honorable than many other brokers, such as banking, insurance, and the stock market. They rely on restrictive state and federal laws to discourage their competition, whereas the pimp can never use the law to safeguard his position.

3

THE MALE CHAUVINIST PIG

The women's liberation movement is an amalgam of different programs and composed of diverse groups with differing aims. The discriminating intellect may accept some of the aims, purposes, motivations, and programs of women's liberation, and reject others. It would be folly to treat as equivalent a host of different values and attitudes merely because they have been packaged together. The views of the women's liberation movement can be divided into four major categories—each of which requires a different approach.

COERCIVE ACTIONS TAKEN AGAINST WOMEN

Apart from murder, the most brutal coercive action taken against women is rape. Yet in this male dominated society rape is not always illegal. It is not illegal when perpetrated upon a woman by her husband. And, although rape is illegal when it occurs outside the "sanctity" of marriage, the way in which it is treated by the law leaves much to be desired. For one thing, if there was any previous acquaintanceship between the rapist and his victim, the court presumes that there was no rape. For another, in order to prove rape, it was necessary in many states until recently, that there be a witness to the crime. Furthermore, if friends of the rapist swore they had sexual intercourse with the victim, she could be characterized as "immoral," and it becomes virtually impossible to obtain a conviction. If the victim is a prostitute, it is equally impossible to obtain a conviction. The reasoning behind the legal inability for a prostitute to be raped is the ludicrous view that it is impossible to compel a person to do that which she does willingly at other times.

One of the most attractive aspects of the women's liberation movement is its support for greater penalties for rape, plus restitution to the victim. Previously people who occupied a comparable position on the political spectrum as do most of today's feminists (e.g., liberals and leftists) urged lighter sentences for rapists and general mollycoddling of criminals. In their view, all crime, rape included, was caused mainly by poverty, family breakdown, lack of recreational facilities, etc. And their "solution" followed directly from this "insight": more welfare, more parks and playgrounds for the underprivileged, counseling, therapy, etc. In contrast, the feminists' insistence on stiffer jail sentences for rapists—and worse—comes like a breath of fresh air.

Although rape is the most striking instance in which the government acquiesces in coercive actions against women, there are others. Consider what is implied by the laws against prostitution. These laws prohibit trade between mutually consenting adults. They are harmful to women in that they prevent them from earning an honest living. If their anti-woman bias is not clear enough, consider the fact that although the transaction is just as illegal for the customer as for the seller, the male (customer) is almost never arrested when the female (seller) is.

Abortion is another case in point. Although inroads have finally been made, abortion is limited by obstructive rules. Both outright prohibition of abortion and abortion under present controls deny the great moral principle of self-ownership. Thus, they are throwbacks to slavery, a situation essentially defined by the barriers put up between people and their right of self-ownership. If a woman owns her body then she owns her womb, and she alone has the complete and sole right to determine whether to have a child or not.

The ways in which the government supports or is itself actively involved in coercing women are manifold. Until very recently, for example, women did not have the same rights as men to own property or to engage in contracts. There are still laws on the books that prevent *married* women, but not married men, from selling property or engaging in business without the permission of their spouses. There are stiffer entrance requirements for women than men at some state universities. The infamous tracking system in our public schools shunts young boys into "male" activities (sports and carpentry), and young girls into "female" activities (cooking and sewing).

It is important to realize that these problems all have two things in common: they are instances of aggressive force used against women and they are all inextricably bound up with the apparatus of the state. Although not widely appreciated, this is no more true of rape and prostitution than of the other actions and activities described. For what does it mean to say that women do not have the right to abort, to own property, or to set up businesses, except that women who engage in these activities will be stopped by state compulsion, fines, or jail sentences.

Clearly, both the government as well as individuals can discriminate. But *only* state and *not* private discrimination violate the rights of women. When a private individual discriminates, he (or she) does so with his (or her) own resources, in his (or her) own name. But when the state discriminates, it does so with resources taken from its citizenry and in the name of all of its subjects. This is a crucial difference.

If a private enterprise such as a movie discriminates, it runs the risk of losing money and possible bankruptcy. People opposing the discrimination may withhold funds or not patronize the institution. However, when the state discriminates, these people do not have this option, and there is no risk of bankruptcy. Even when people oppose discrimination in a state institution from which they can withhold funds, (students can, for example, at a state university) the state has other alternatives. It can make up for the dwindling funds from tax revenues, and these must be paid under threat of compulsion.

Even the pinches that women are subject to are inextricably bound up with the state apparatus. Contrast what happens when sexual harassment takes place *within* the confines of a private place (a department store) and when it takes place *outside* (on a street one block away from the store). When a woman is molested within the confines of a private place the whole force of the profit-and-loss free-enterprise system comes to bear on the problem. It is in the entrepreneur's self-interest to apprehend and discourage offensive actions. If he does not, he will lose customers. There is, in effect, competition between store owners to provide safe and comfortable environments for customers. The ones who succeed to the greatest degree in their antipinching drive will tend to reap the greatest profits. The ones who fail, whether because they ignore the issue or are unsuccessful in implementing their programs, will tend to incur the greatest losses. This, of course, is not a guarantee that pinching and other offensive behavior will cease. It will always occur as long as people remain imperfectly moral. But this system does encourage, by profits and losses, those who are most able to control the situation.

Contrasted with what occurs in the public domain, however, the private system begins to look like perfection itself. In the public domain there is almost no incentive to deal with the problem. There is no one who *automatically* loses anything when a woman is pinched or otherwise harassed. The city police are supposedly charged with the responsibility, but they function without benefit of the automatic profit-and-loss incentive system. Their salaries which are paid for by taxation, are not related to performance and they suffer no financial loss when women are molested. It is clear then why most of this type of harassment occurs on the streets and not within shops and stores.

NONCOERCIVE ACTIONS TAKEN AGAINST WOMEN

Many actions taken against women are not, strictly speaking, coercive. For example, whistling, leering, derision, innuendo, unwelcome flirtation, etc. (Of course, it is often difficult to tell beforehand whether a flirtatious remark will be welcome or not.) Consider the sexual come-ons which continually occur between men and women. Although to many people, and especially those in the women's movement, there is no real difference between this type of behavior and coercive acts, the distinction is crucial. Both may be objectionable to many women, but one is a physically invasive act, the other is not.

There are many other kinds of actions which fall into the same category. Examples include the use of sexual vulgarisms ("broad" or "piece of ass"), the advocacy of double-standard mores, certain rules of etiquette, the encouragement of the mental capacity of boys and not of girls, the societal opprobrium of women who participate in "male" athletic activities, "sexist" advertising, and the pedestals that women are placed upon.

There are two important points to be made with regard to these and other attitudes and behavior which may be offensive but not coercive. The first is that such noncoercive actions cannot legitimately be outlawed. Any attempt to do so would involve the mass violation of the rights of other individuals. Freedom of speech means that people have the right to say whatever they like, even to make possibly reprehensible and boorish statements.

The second point is more complicated and by no means obvious. To a considerable extent, these reprehensible but noncoercive actions are themselves fostered and encouraged by *coercive* statist activities which operate behind-the-scenes. For example, the widespread incidence of government ownership and management of land, parks, sidewalks, roads, businesses, etc. These coercive activities, based on illegitimate compulsory taxation, can be legitimately criticized. If they were eliminated, the unsavory but legal behavior they support would diminish, with the aid of the free market.

Consider as an example the case in which a (male) boss harasses a (female) secretary in an objectionable but noncoercive manner. We shall compare the situation when such activity takes place on public and private property. To analyze this, we must understand what the labor economist calls "compensating differentials." A compensating differential is the amount of money just necessary to compensate an employee for the psychic losses that go with the job. For instance, suppose there are two job opportunities. One is in an air-conditioned office, with a good view, pleasant surroundings and pleasant coworkers. The other is in a damp basement, surrounded by hostile fellow workers. However, there is usually *some* wage differential large enough to attract an individual to the less pleasant job. The exact amount of the differential varies for different people. But it exists.

Just as a compensating differential must be paid to hire employees to work in damp basements, so it must be paid to female workers in offices where they are subject to sexual harassment. This increase in wages comes out of the boss's pocket if he is a private businessman. Thus he has a strong monetary incentive to control his behavior and the behavior of those who work for him.

But the increase in wages is not paid by the boss of a government or government-supported enterprise! It is paid by the taxpayer's money, which is not paid upon the deliverance of satisfactory services, but is collected by coercion. Thus the boss has less reason to exercise control. It is clear that this type of sexual harassment, in itself offensive but not coercive, is made possible by the coercive actions of the government in its role as tax collector. If taxes were paid voluntarily, the boss, even in a government office, would be subject to meaningful control. He would stand to lose money if his behavior offended his employees. But because he is supported by money from coercive taxation, his employees are at his mercy.

In like manner, contrast the situation where a group of men whistle, jeer, and make disparaging and insulting remarks to and about women passersby. One group does this on a publicly owned sidewalk or street, the other in a privately owned place such as a restaurant or shopping mall.

Now, under which condition is this legal but reprehensible behavior more likely to be ended? In the public sector, it is in no businessperson's financial interest to end the harassment. Since

"This is mission control—Houston advises that Astronaut Mary Ellen Wilson is 26 hours into her menstrual cycle with only occasional bursts of anger directed toward Lt. Commander Joe Farley and Captain Ed Veidt interspersed with moderate sobbing."

by assumption this behavior is legal, the public police forces cannot do anything to stop it either.

But in the realm of private enterprise, every entrepreneur who hopes to employ or sell to women (or to men who object to this maltreatment of women) has a strong pecuniary incentive to end it. This is why it is no accident that such harassment almost always takes place on public sidewalks or streets, and virtually never in department stores, restaurants, shopping malls, or other establishments which seek profits and care about their bottom line.

THE MALE CHAUVINIST PIG AS HERO

Consideration in some detail should be given to two grievous errors committed by the adherents of women's liberation. It is for his good sense in opposing these programs that the male chauvinist pig can be considered a hero.

Laws compelling "equal wages for equal work." The question is, of course, how to define "equal work." If "equal work" is taken literally, it embraces all aspects of the employee's productivity in the short run as well as in the long run, including psychic differentials, the discrimination of customers and other workers, and the ability of the employee to mesh with the likes, dislikes, and idiosyncrasies of the entrepreneur. In short, all these components must be weighted, if equal work is exactly the same as equal profitability for the entrepreneur. Only then, in the free market, workers with such equal abilities will tend to earn equal wages. If, for instance, women were paid less than men even though they were equally good workers in this sense, forces would be set up which, when carried to their conclusion, would insure equal pay. How? The employer would be able to make more money by replacing male workers with female workers. The demand for male workers would decrease, thus lowering male wages, and the demand for female workers would increase, raising female wages. Every employer who substituted a woman for a man would have a competitive advantage over the one who refused to do so. The profit maximizing employers would continually earn greater profits than would the discriminatory employers. The profit maximizers would be able to undersell the discriminators, and, other things being equal, eventually drive them into bankruptcy.

In actual point of fact, however, the proponents of equal wages for equal work do not have this strict type of equality in mind. Their definition of "equality" is equal years of schooling, equivalent skills, equivalent college degrees, and perhaps similar scores in qualification tests. However, individuals who are virtually identical with respect to such criteria can have vastly different abilities to earn profits for employers. For example, consider two workers, one male, one female, identical as far as test scores and college degrees are concerned. It is an indisputable fact that in the event of a pregnancy, it is far more likely for the woman to stay home and raise the child. Consideration of whether this custom is *fair* or not is not relevant. What is pertinent is whether it is *factual* or not. If the woman stays at home, interrupting a career or employment, she will be worth less to the employer. In this case, although the male and female candidates for the job might be identically qualified, in the long run, the man will be more productive than the woman and, therefore, more valuable to the employer.

Paradoxically, many pieces of evidence which indicate that men and women are not equally productive come from the women's liberation movement itself. There are several studies in which women and men were first tested as groups, in isolation from one another, and then together, in competition with one another. In some cases, when the groups were tested in isolation, the women showed clearly that they had higher innate abilities than the men. Yet, when the two groups were tested in competition, the men invariably scored better than the women. Again, it should be emphasized that the concern here is not with the *fairness* of such occurrences, but with the *effects*. The point is that in the world of work, women will often find themselves in competition with men. If they constantly defer to men, and cannot do their best in competition with men, they are, in fact, of less help in procuring profits for the entrepreneur. If women are equal to men in test scores and are inferior to them when it comes to profit maximizing, then the equal pay for equal work law will prove disastrous for women.

It will be calamitous because the profit maximizing incentives will be turned around. Instead of the market exerting a strong steady push toward firing men and hiring women, employers will be motivated to fire women and hire men in their place. If he is forced to pay men and women the same wages, even though they are not equally productive, profits will be increased to the degree that male workers replace females. Employers who are inclined to take the feminist view, and insist on keeping woman workers, will have decreased profits, and lose their share of the market. The employers who prosper will be those who do not hire women.

It should be stressed that the tendency for women who are truly equal to men in productivity to receive equal wages exists only in the profit-and-loss free market. Only in free enterprise are there financial incentives to hire highly productive under-priced women, to "take advantage" of their plight, and thus to raise their wages.

In the government and nonprofit sectors, these profit incentives are, by definition, absent. It is hardly an accident, then, that virtually all real abuses of women in this respect take place in government and nonprofit areas such as schools, universities, libraries, foundations, social work, and public services. There are few allegations of underpayment to women in private enterprise fields such as computers, advertising, or the media.

LAWS COMPELLING NONDISCRIMINATION

McSorley's is a bar in New York City that catered exclusively to men, until it was "liberated." Under the banner of the new antidiscrimination law in New York State, women were served for the first time in the history of the establishment. This was hailed as a great progressive step forward by liberal, progressive, and women's liberation factions. The basic philosophy behind the law and the attendant liberation of McSorley's seems to be that it is illegitimate to discriminate between potential customers on the basis of sex.

If the problems with this philosophy are not readily apparent, they can be made so by considering several *reductiones ad absurdum*. If the philosophy were strictly adhered to, for example, would not separate bathrooms for men at "public" places be considered "discriminatory"? And separate residence halls for men? What about male homosexuals? They could be accused of "discrimination" against women. And aren't the women who marry men discriminating against other women?

These examples, of course, are ridiculous. But they are consistent with the philosophy of antidiscrimination. If they are ridiculous, it is because that philosophy is ridiculous.

It is important to realize that *all* human actions imply discrimination in the only sensible definition of that much abused term: picking and choosing from available alternatives, the one which best serves his or her interests. There is no action taken by human beings which fails to accord with this dictum. We discriminate when we choose a toothpaste, decide upon a means of transportation, whom to marry. The discrimination practiced by the gourmet or wine taster is and can only be the discrimination practiced by all human beings. Any attack upon discrimination, therefore, is an attempt to restrict the options open to all individuals.

But what of the women's option to drink at McSorley's? Was their right to choose being violated? No. What they experienced was what a man experiences when a woman rejects his sexual advances. The woman who refuses to date a man is not guilty of violating his rights—for his rights do not include a relationship with her. That exists as a possibility, but not a right, unless she is his slave. In the same way, a man who wishes to drink in the company of other men is not guilty of violating women's rights. For women's rights do not include drinking with people who do not wish to drink with them. It is only in a slave society that this is not so. It is only in a slave society that the master can compel the slave to do his bidding. If the antidiscriminatory forces succeed in forcing their philosophy on the general public they will also succeed in forcing on the public the cloven hoof of slavery. To the extent that the male chauvinist pig succeeds in resisting these trends, he must be looked upon as a hero.

II. MEDICAL

4

THE DRUG PUSHER

The drug business, an evil business, is responsible for ago-nizing deaths, crime, robbery, enforced prostitution, and often murder. The addict is usually marked for life, even after "kicking the habit." During the addictive period, the addict is a helpless slave to the drug, willing to enter into any degrada-tion to secure "one more fix."

How then can the evil nature of the drug pusher be ques-tioned? How can we even presume to look upon him with favor?

The evils commonly blamed on heroin addiction are in real-ity the fault of the *prohibition* of drugs and not of the addiction itself. Given the prohibition of drugs, it is the person who sells drugs illegally who does more than anyone to *mitigate* the evil effects of the original prohibition.

The prohibition of heroin has the devastating effect of forc-ing the price up to a level which can only be characterized as astronomical. When a commodity is outlawed, in addition to all the usual costs of growing, harvesting, curing, transporting, merchandising, etc., the costs of evading the law and paying for the punishments meted out when the evasion fails, must be added. In the case of bootleg whiskey (during the prohibition era of the 20s), these extra costs were not excessive because law enforcement was lax and the legislation did not have widespread popular support. In the case of heroin, these costs are enormous. Anti-heroin legislation enjoys wide popular support, with demands for even stricter laws and penalties. Vigilante groups and youth gangs in the inner city ghetto areas have inflicted their own punishment on drug pushers and addicts. These groups have had the quasi-support of the "law and order" faction, making it difficult and expensive to bribe the police who fear the great penalties society would impose on them if they were caught.

In addition to having to pay costly bribes to the police, the drug merchants must also pay high salaries to their employees for the dangers they encounter in smuggling and operating the factories which prepare the drugs for street sales. They must also exercise a degree of paternalism in taking care of those employees who are caught bribing politicians, lawyers, and judges to minimize the penalties.

These are the factors which account for the high price of heroin. But for these many extra costs imposed by the prohibition of heroin, the price would not differ in any significant way from the price of other crops (wheat, tobacco, soya beans, etc.). If heroin were legalized, an addict could obtain his daily need for about the cost of a loaf of bread, according to the best estimates.

Under prohibition, heroin addiction may cost as much as $100 per day for a mature habit. Depending upon market information and alternative sources of supply, the addict spends about $35,000 per year to support his habit. It is obvious that *this cost* is responsible for the untold human suffering usually blamed on heroin addiction. The typical addict is usually young, uneducated, and unable to earn a sufficient amount of money by honest means to support his habit. If he does not seek medical and psychiatric help, the only choice the addict can make to secure his "fix" is to enter into a life of crime where he may eventually be hunted down by the police or street gangs. Furthermore, the addict criminal is in a far worse position than the nonaddict. The nonaddict criminal can select the most opportune time and place for a robbery. But the addict must commit a crime whenever he needs a "fix," and these times usually occur when his reactions are dulled by his drug deprivation.

In reflecting upon the economics of "fencing" stolen merchandise, it becomes obvious that the addict must commit an enormous amount of crime to support his habit. To have the annual amount of $35,000 necessary to buy drugs, the addict must steal roughly *five times* that amount (almost $200,000 per year), since the buyers of stolen merchandise (fences), usually pay only 20 percent or less of the retail value of what they buy. If the figure of $200,000 is multiplied by the estimated 10,000 addicts in New York City, the total of $20 billion is the amount of the total value lost in crimes committed by addicts in the Big Apple.

It cannot be stressed strongly enough that these crimes are due to the *prohibition of heroin* and not the result of heroin addiction. It is the prohibition that drastically forces its price up and drives the addict into a life of crime and brutishness which may end in his own death or that of the victim.

To prove this point, consider the small but significant number of medical doctors who, having access to heroin, have addicted themselves. Its price is not prohibitive since their supply of the drug is not illegal. Their lives are "normal," useful, and fulfilling—with just this one difference. Economically speaking, their lives would not be too different if, instead of being addicted to heroin, they were diabetics and addicted to insulin. With either addiction, these doctors would still be able to function professionally. If, however, their legal supply of heroin were cut off (or insulin were suddenly declared illegal), these doctors would be at the mercy of the street pusher, unable to ascertain the quality of the drugs they purchased, and forced to pay exorbitant prices for their supply. Under these changed circumstances the position of the addicted doctor would be more difficult, but it would not be catastrophic, since most of these professionals could easily afford the $35,000 annual cost of their habit. But what of the uneducated addict living in poverty, who does not have these prospects?

The *function* of the heroin seller, as opposed to his motivation in entering the field, is to keep the price of the drug *down*. Each time a few more heroin sellers enter the industry, the price goes down even more. Conversely, each time the number of heroin sellers decreases (through discouragement or prosecution), the price rises. Since it is not the sale or use of heroin itself that is responsible for the plight of the addict or for the crimes he commits, but rather the *high price of heroin* caused by its prohibition, it must follow that any action which results in a drop in the price of the drug alleviates the problem. If the problem is caused by the high cost of the drug, then lowering the cost must be considered as a solution.

But it is the heroin pusher who is instrumental in lowering the price of the drug, and the forces of "law and order" who are responsible for raising these prices by interfering with the activities of the pusher. Therefore, it is the much reviled drug dealer, not the widely beloved narcotics agent ("narc"), who must be considered the heroic figure.

Legalization of heroin has been rejected on the grounds that progress and civilization would come to a halt. The British and Chinese experience with addictive drugs are cited, and we are supposed to picture scores of people lying around in the street, zonked out of their minds. The argument is that anything which interferes with progress, such as the widespread use of heroin, should be prohibited. But there are other things that can interfere with continued progress which most people would not be willing to prohibit—leisure, for one. If employees took vacations which amounted to 90 percent of the working year, "progress" would certainly falter. Should long vacations be prohibited? Hardly. In addition, the present prohibition of heroin does not eliminate access to the drug. Formerly, it was available only in the inner city ghettos; today it can be purchased on affluent suburban street corners and schoolyards.

In the example of the Chinese experience with drugs, Chinese merchants were *forced* by gun boat "diplomacy" to accept opium. The legalization of addictive drugs would in no way *force* individuals into the habit. Indeed, force, or the elimination of force, is the chief reason for scrapping the prohibition of heroin.

In the British case (drugs administered legally, at a low cost, by a doctor or licensed clinic), the argument has been made that the number of addicts has risen sharply since their low cost program started. But this rise is a statistical artifact. Formerly, many people were reluctant to report themselves as addicts when it was illegal to be one. When addiction was legalized and low cost drugs were available, the statistics naturally rose. The British Government Health Service administers drugs to certified addicts *only*. It would, indeed, be surprising if there were any marked increase in the rate of addiction under these circumstances.

Another source of the increase in the number of statistically *counted* addicts is the migration to the United Kingdom from Commonwealth countries. This sudden immigration might well cause temporary problems of adjustment, but it is hardly an indictment of the British plan. On the contrary, it provides ample testimony to the farsightedness and progressiveness of the program. To blame this program for the rise in addiction would be similar to blaming Dr. Christiaan Barnard (the first doctor to perform transplant heart surgery) for the rise in the number of people in South Africa who wanted heart surgery.

In conclusion, it should be stated that heroin addiction may be an unmitigated evil, without any socially redeeming features. If so, efforts to publicize the evils of addiction can only be applauded. However, the present prohibition of heroin and other hard drugs serves no useful purpose. It has caused a countless amount of suffering, and great social upheaval. In seeking to uphold this vicious law, the narcotics agent keeps prices up and adds to the tragedy. It is only the heroin seller, by acting so as to lower prices, even at considerable personal risk, who saves lives and alleviates the tragedy somewhat.

5

THE DRUG ADDICT

At the present time, with the intense discussion on the evils of heroin addiction, it is well to heed the old adage—"listen to both sides of the story." Among the many reasons for this, and perhaps most important, is the fact that if everyone is against something (particularly heroin addiction), one can assume that there is *something* which can be said in its favor. Throughout mankind's long and disputatious history, the majority opinion has, the majority of times, been wrong.

On the other hand, even those who agree with the majority opinion should also welcome an attack upon it. The best way to teach the verities of life, according to the Utilitarian John Stuart Mill, is by hearing the opposition. Let the position be challenged, and let the challenge fail. This method was considered by Mill to be so important that he recommended inventing a challenging position, if a real one was not forthcoming, and presenting it as convincingly as possible. Thus, those who believe in the unmitigated evils of heroin addiction should be eager to hear an argument in favor of it.

The phenomenon of addiction should be considered from an intrinsic point of view. That is, the assumption will be that the social or interpersonal problem—the necessity for an addict to become involved in criminal activities in order to support his

"To be honest with you I'm very much satisfied with the quality of drugs from the pharmaceutical house I deal with now."

habit—has been solved. For this is caused by the legislation which prohibits the sale of narcotic drugs, and thus is a problem extrinsic to the drug itself. The intrinsic problems of addiction are all the other problems addicts are alleged to face.

Primary on any list of the nonsocial problems of drug addiction is the allegation that addiction shortens life. Depending on the age and health of the addict, and the pessimism or optimism of the alleger, the figure by which life is said to be shortened varies between 10 and 40 years. This is indeed unfortunate, but it hardly constitutes a valid criticism of addiction, and it most certainly does not justify the prohibition of heroin use.

It does not constitute a valid criticism or justify prohibition because it is up to the individual to determine the kind of life he will lead—a short one, including what he considers to be pleasurable activities, or a longer one, without such enjoyment. Since there is no objective criterion for such choices, there is nothing irrational or even suspect about any choice on the spectrum. One may choose to maximize the possibility of longevity, even if this means the renunciation of liquor, tobacco, gambling, sex, travel, crossing the street, heated debate, and strenuous exercise. Or, one may choose to engage in any or all of these activities, even if that means a shortened lifespan.

Another argument leveled against addiction is that it prevents people from fulfilling their responsibilities. The example usually given is that of a father who, under the continuous influence of heroin, becomes incapable of fulfilling his financial and other obligations to his family. Let us assume that heroin addiction incapacitates the father. It still does not follow that the use and sale of heroin should be prohibited. It would be unreasonable to prohibit any activity on the grounds that it prevents some people from functioning in certain ways. Why should the people who are not impaired or who do not have like responsibilities be restricted? Were it proper to prohibit heroin for this reason, surely it would also be proper to prohibit gambling, drinking, smoking, automobile driving, air travel, and other dangerous or potentially dangerous activities. But this would be patently absurd.

Should heroin be legal for some people but not for the others who do not accept or fulfill their responsibilities because of their addiction? No. When a man, to continue the example, marries, he does not agree to renounce all activities which might be dangerous. The marriage contract is not, after all, a slave contract. Marriage does not prevent either party from engaging in activities which might discomfort the other. People with responsibilities do get heart attacks from playing tennis. But no one would suggest that people with responsibilities be barred from sports activities.

Another argument against drug addiction is the claim that users become totally nonproductive and thus, as a group, lower the GNP (Gross National Product)—an index of the economic well-being of the country as a whole. Thus, the argument runs, drug addiction hurts the country.

The argument is specious, because it considers the country's well-being a meaningful concept, rather than the addict's. But even in its own terms, it is not convincing. It is based upon an equation of the GNP with economic well-being. And this equation is fallacious. The GNP, for example, counts all government spending as contributing to the well-being of the country, whether it actually does so or not. It fails to take into account the work of housewives done in the home. Furthermore, it completely miscontrues the economic status of leisure. Any assessment of economic well-being must assign some value to leisure, but the GNP does not. For example, the GNP should double with the introduction and full-time implementation of an invention which allowed people to double their output of real goods and services. But if the people *choose* to use the invention to just maintain their standard of living and instead halve their workday, the GNP would not change by one iota.

It is true that if addiction to heroin leads to increased leisure, it will cause a fall in the GNP. But an increase in leisure *for any reason* will have the same effect. Therefore, if we oppose addiction on this ground, we must also oppose enjoyable vacations, poetic contemplation, and walks in the woods. The list of proscribed activities could be endless. There is nothing wrong with choosing to utilize an increase in wealth by increasing one's leisure. And if the GNP decreases thereby, so much the worse for the GNP.

Finally, it is by no means clear that addiction necessarily leads to lessened economic activity. Most of our knowledge about the behavior of addicts comes from the study of those who, because of legislation which prohibits heroin and, therefore, skyrockets its price, must spend most of their time in an agonizing search for vast sums of money. They cannot hold traditional jobs because most of their time is spent stealing, murdering, and prostituting. Since we are concentrating on the personal problem of addiction and not on the social problem, the evidence afforded by these people is irrelevant to the discussion. To study the behavior of addicts who are not prohibited by law from being productive, we must turn to those few addicts who are lucky enough to be insured a steady supply of low-cost heroin.

This group is composed mainly of doctors who can use their prescription-writing powers to insure themselves a steady supply. The limited evidence furnished by this small sample seems to indicate that addicts, freed from the compulsions induced by heroin prohibition, are able to lead rather normal and productive lives. The doctors in question provide service as adequately as other doctors. From all indications, they are able to keep up with the latest developments in their field, maintain a proper relationship with their patients, and function no differently, in all relevant aspects, from other physicians.

To be sure, were heroin legal, addicts would continue to have drug-related personal problems. There would be the fear of possible renewal of prohibition, and the relative incapacitation following the periods of drug use. There would be the danger of overdosing, although it would lessen under legalization, since the drug could be administered under the supervision of a doctor. Vestiges of the old prohibitory attitude might remain and manifest themselves in the form of prejudice against addicts.

The point to be stressed, however, is not that addicts will have drug-related problems even under legalization. Special problems almost always accompany special interests; violin players are always in fear of injuring their fingers and ballerinas cannot afford stubbed toes. Addiction to heroin is not in and of itself an evil. If it is legalized, it cannot possibly hurt anyone but the user of the drug. There are those who may want to speak out, educate, and advertise against it, but to prohibit it is clearly a violation of the rights of those who wish to use it.

III. FREE SPEECH

6

THE BLACKMAILER

At first glance it is not hard to answer the question, "Is blackmail really illegitimate?" The only problem it would seem to pose is, "Why is it being asked at all?" Do not blackmailers, well . . . *blackmail* people? And what could be worse? Blackmailers prey on people's dark hidden secrets. They threaten to expose and publicize them. They bleed their victims, and often drive them to suicide.

We will find, however, that the case against the blackmailer cannot stand serious analysis; that it is based upon a tissue of unexamined shibboleths and deep philosophical misunderstandings.

What, exactly, is blackmail? Blackmail is the *offer* of trade. It is the offer to trade something, usually *silence*, for some other good, usually money. If the offer of the trade is *accepted*, the blackmailer then maintains his silence and the blackmailee pays the agreed-upon price. If the blackmail offer is *rejected*, the blackmailer may exercise his rights of free speech and publicize the secret. There is nothing amiss here. All that is happening is that an *offer* to maintain silence is being made. If the offer is rejected, the blackmailer does no more than exercise his right of free speech.

"This is my kid, Mr. T. He'll be blackmailing you from now on —I'm retiring to Florida."

The sole difference between a gossip and a blackmailer is that the blackmailer will refrain from speaking—for a price. In a sense, the gossip is much *worse* than the blackmailer, for the blackmailer has given the blackmailee a chance to silence him. The gossip exposes the secret without warning. Is not the person with a secret better off at the hands of a blackmailer than a gossip? With the gossip, all is lost; with the blackmailer, one can only gain, or at least be no worse off. If the price requested by the blackmailer is lower than the secret is worth, the secretholder will pay the blackmailer—this being the lesser of the two evils. He thus *gains* the difference to him between the value of the secret and the price of the blackmail. When the blackmailer demands more than the secret is worth, his demand will not be met and the information will become public. However, in this case the person is no worse off with the blackmailer than he would have been with the inveterate gossip. It is indeed difficult, then, to account for the vilification suffered by the blackmailer, at least compared to the gossip, who is usually dismissed with slight contempt and smugness.

Blackmail need not entail the offer of *silence* in return for *money*. This is only the best known form. But blackmail may be defined without reference to either. Defined in general terms, blackmail is the threat to do something—anything which is not in itself illegal—unless certain demands are met.

Many actions in the public arena qualify as acts of blackmail, but, instead of being vilified, they have often attained a status of respectability! For example, the recent lettuce boycott is a form of blackmail. Through the lettuce boycott (or any boycott) *threats are made* to retailers and wholesalers of fruits and vegetables. If they handle nonunion lettuce, the boycotters assert, people will be asked not to patronize their establishments. This conforms perfectly to the definition: a threat that something, not in itself illegal, will take place unless certain demands are met.

But what about the *threats* involved in blackmail? This perhaps more than anything else, is the aspect of blackmail that is most misunderstood and feared. At first glance, one is inclined to agree that threats are immoral. The usual dictum against aggression, for example, warns not only against aggression *per se* but also against *the threat of aggression*. If a highwayman accosts a traveler, it is usually the *threat* of aggression alone that will compel obedience.

Consider the nature of threats. When what is threatened is aggressive violence, the threat is condemnable. No individual has the right to initiate aggressive violence against another. In blackmail, however, what is being "threatened" is something that the blackmailer *does* have a right to do!—whether it be exercising the right of free speech, or refusing to patronize certain stores, or persuading others to do likewise. What is being threatened is not in itself illegitimate; it is, therefore, not possible to call the "threat" an *illegitimate threat.*

Blackmail can only be illegitimate when there is a special foresworn relationship between the blackmailer and the blackmailee. A secret-keeper may take a lawyer or a private investigator into his confidence *on the condition that the confidence be maintained in secrecy.* If the lawyer or private investigator attempts to blackmail the secret-keeper, that would be in violation of the contract and, *therefore*, illegitimate. However, if a stranger holds the secret without contractual obligations, then it is legitimate to offer to "sell" his silence.

In addition to being a legitimate activity, blackmail has some good effects, litanies to the contrary notwithstanding. Apart from some innocent victims who are caught in the net, whom does the blackmailer usually prey upon? In the main, there are two groups. One group is composed of criminals: murderers, thieves, swindlers, embezzlers, cheaters, rapists, etc. The other group consists of people who engage in activities, not illegitimate in themselves, but which are contrary to the mores and habits of the majority: homosexuals, sado-masochists, sexual perverts, communists, adulterers, etc. The institution of blackmail has beneficial, but different, effects upon each of these groups.

In the case of criminals, blackmail and the threat of blackmail serves as a deterrent. They add to the risks involved in criminal activity. How many of the anonymous "tips" received by the police—the value of which cannot be overestimated—can be traced, directly or indirectly, to blackmail? How many criminals are led to pursue crime on their own, eschewing the aid of fellow criminals in "jobs" that call for cooperation, out of the fear of possible blackmail? Finally, there are those individuals who are on the verge of committing crimes, or at the "margin of criminality" (as the economist would say), where the least factor will propel them one way or another. The additional fear of blackmail may be enough, in some cases, to dissuade them from crime.

If blackmail itself were legalized, it would undoubtedly be an even more effective deterrent. Legalization would undoubtedly result in an increase in blackmail, with attendant depredations upon the criminal class.

It is sometimes said that what diminishes crime is not the penalty attached to the crime but the certainty of being caught. Although this controversy rages with great relevance in current debates on capital punishment, it will suffice to point out that the institution of blackmail does both. It increases the penalty associated with crime, as it forces criminals to share part of their loot with the blackmailer. It also raises the probability of being apprehended, as blackmailers are added to police forces, private citizen and vigilante groups, and other anticrime units. Blackmailers, who are often members in good standing in the criminal world, are in an advantageous position to foil crimes. Their "inside" status surpasses even that of the spy or infiltrator, who is forced to play a role. Legalizing blackmail would thus allow anticrime units to take advantage of two basic crime fighting adages at the same time: "divide and conquer," and "lack of honor among thieves." It is quite clear that one important effect of legalizing blackmail would be to diminish crime, real crime, that is.

The legalization of blackmail would also have a beneficial effect upon actions which do not involve aggression, but are at variance with the mores of society as a whole. On these actions, the legalization of blackmail would have a liberating effect. Even with blackmail still illegal, we are witnessing some of its beneficial effects. Homosexuality, for instance, is technically illegal in some instances, but not really criminal, since it involves no aggression. For *individual* homosexuals, blackmail very often causes considerable harm and can hardly be considered beneficial. But for the group as a whole, that is, *for each individual as a member of the group*, blackmail has helped by making the public more aware and accustomed to homosexuality. Forcing individual members of a socially oppressed group into the open, or "out of the closet," cannot, of course, be considered a service. The use of force is a violation of an individual's rights. But still, it does engender an awareness on the part of members of a group of one another's existence. In forcing this perception, blackmail can legitimately take some small share of the credit in liberating people whose only crime is a deviation from the norm in a noncriminal way.

In reflecting on the old aphorism, "the truth shall make you free," the only "weapon" at the disposal of the blackmailer is the truth. In using the truth to back up his threats (as on occasion he must), he sets the truth free, very often without intent, to do whatever good or bad it is capable of doing.

7

THE SLANDERER AND LIBELER

It is easy to be an advocate of free speech when it applies to the rights of those with whom one is in agreement. But the crucial test concerns controversial speech—statements which we may consider vicious and nasty and which may, in fact, even *be* vicious and nasty.

Now, there is perhaps nothing more repugnant or vicious than libel. We must, therefore, take particular care to defend the free speech rights of libelers, for if they can be protected, the rights of all others—who do not give as much offense—will certainly be more secure. But if the rights of free speech of libelers and slanderers are not protected, the rights of others will be less secure.

The reason civil libertarians have not been involved in the protection of the rights of libelers and slanderers is clear—libel is ruinous to reputations. Harsh tales about lost jobs, friends, etc., abound. Far from being concerned with the free speech rights of the libeler and slanderer, civil libertarians have been concerned with protecting those who have had their reputations destroyed, as though that in itself was unpardonable. But obviously, protecting a person's reputation is not an absolute value. If it were, if, that is, reputations were really sacrosanct, then we

"*This is calumny, slander! You'll hear from my attorney—I spent years building up the reputation of my restaurant!*"

would have to prohibit most categories of denigration, even truthful ones. Unfavorable literary criticism, satire in movies, plays, music or book reviews could not be allowed. Anything which diminished any individual's or any institution's reputation would have to be forbidden.

Of course, civil libertarians would deny that their objection to slander and libel commits them to the view described. They would admit that a person's reputation cannot always be protected, that sometimes it must be sacrificed. But this, they might say, does not exonerate the libeler. For a person's reputation is not something to be taken lightly. It may not be damaged without good reason.

But what is a person's "reputation"? What is this thing which may not be "taken lightly"? Clearly, it is not a possession which may be said to belong to him in the way, for example, his clothes do. In fact, a person's reputation does not "belong" to him at all. A person's reputation is *what other people think of him*; it *consists* of the thoughts which *other* people have.

A man does not *own* his reputation any more than he owns the thoughts of others—because that is all his reputation consists of. A man's reputation cannot be stolen from him any more than can the thoughts of *other* people be stolen from *him*. Whether his reputation was "taken from him" by fair means or foul, by truth or falsehood, he did not own it in the first place and, hence, should have no recourse to the law for damages.

What then are we doing when we object to, or prohibit, libel? We are prohibiting someone from affecting or trying to affect the *thoughts of other* people. But what does the right of free speech mean if not that we are all free to try to affect the thoughts of those around us? So we must conclude that libel and slander are consistent with the rights of free speech.

Finally, paradoxical though it may be, reputations would probably be more secure without the laws which prohibit libelous speech! With the present laws prohibiting libelous falsehoods, there is a natural tendency to *believe* any publicized slur on someone's character. "It would not be printed if it were not true," reasons the gullible public. If libel and slander were allowed, however, the public would not be so easily deceived. Attacks would come so thick and fast that they would have to be *substantiated* before they could have any impact. Agencies similar to Consumers Union or the Better Business Bureau might be

8

THE DENIER OF ACADEMIC FREEDOM

More crocodile tears have been shed over the issue of academic freedom than perhaps any other. Academics are possibly more eloquent on this freedom than any other topic receiving their attention. In the eyes of some, it seems to be equated with the very basis of Western civilization! Hardly a day passes without indignant statements from the American Civil Liberties Union over some real or imagined violation of academic freedom. And all this seems pale in comparison with the anger of the labor unions of professional academics and teachers.

From the name itself, academic freedom would seem to be innocuous enough. Certainly "academics," like everyone else, should have freedom—freedom of speech, freedom to travel, freedom to take or leave a job—the usual freedoms that everyone enjoys. But that is not what is meant by the phrase "academic freedom." Instead, it has a very special meaning—the freedom to teach the subject matter in whatever form the academic wishes to teach it, despite any wishes to the contrary his employer may harbor. Therefore, "academic freedom" prohibits the employer from firing the teacher as long as he teaches the subject matter, no matter how objectionable the teaching is.

"Please understand, Professor Rand, we are not questioning your academic freedom. We're just curious. As a favor could you fill us in a trifle about your course, 'John Wayne, Father of Nato'."

Now this is a very special and spectacular doctrine. Consider what would happen if it were applied to almost any other occupation—sanitation work or plumbing. "Plumber's freedom" would consist of the right to install pipes and plumbing equipment in a way the plumber thought best. What if a customer wanted his plumbing done in a way which differed with the plumber's professional judgment. Without the doctrine of "plumber's freedom" the plumber would, of course, be free to refuse the job. But under the doctrine of "plumber's freedom," he would not have to turn it down. He would have the right to take the job and do it *his* way. He would have the right to say that his views should prevail, and the customer would not have the right to dismiss him.

"Taxi driver's freedom," would guarantee to drivers the right to go where *they* wanted to go, regardless of where the paying customer wanted to be taken. "Waiter's freedom," would give the waiter the right to decide what *you* will eat. Why should not plumbers, waiters, and taxi drivers have a "vocational freedom"? Why should it be reserved for academics?

Basically, the difference which is said to exist between these vocations and the academics is that the academics *require* free inquiry, untrammeled rights of expression, and the right to pursue thoughts wherever they may lead. This claim and this distinction is, of course, made by the academics. In addition to being objectionably elitist, this argument also misses an important point, one which is not concerned with the question, of what is involved in intellectual activity. It is the impropriety of "vocational freedom" in upholding the employee's "right" to a job on the basis of purely formalistic requirements, *regardless of the wishes and desires of customers and employers.*

If there is an acceptance of the elitist argument which claims that the "intellectual" professions must be granted a freedom inappropriate to other professions, what of others which qualify as "intellectual"? What about "medical freedom" for doctors, "legal freedom" for lawyers, "artistic freedom" for artists, etc. "Medical freedom" might give doctors the right to perform operations, regardless of whether the patient approved. Would it prevent patients from firing doctors whose procedures they disapproved of? Would "artist freedom" give artists the right to charge for art which is neither wanted nor appreciated? Considering the way "academic freedom" operates, these questions must all

be answered affirmatively. One shudders at the possibility that
these freedoms be granted to chemists, lawyers, or politicians.

What is really at issue in the question of "academic freedom" is the right of individuals to freely contract with one
another. The doctrine of academic freedom is a denial of the
sanctity of contract. The odds are against the employer, and
freezes the situation in favor of the academic. It resembles nothing so much as a medieval guild system, with its restrictions,
protectionism, and the fostering of a caste system.

Thus far, it has been implicitly assumed that the schools and
universities are privately owned. The contention has been that
academic freedom amounts to a violation of the rights of these
property owners.

But virtually all of the institutions of learning in the United
States are controlled by the government, i.e., they are stolen
property. Academic freedom, therefore may be defended on the
ground that it is perhaps the only device by which control over
the educational system may be wrested away, at least in part,
from the ruling class or power elite, which controls it.[1] Assuming that this claim is true, for the sake of argument, there is a
powerful defense of academic freedom.

In this view, it would not be the innocent student-consumer
who is being defrauded by claims to academic freedom; for it is
not the innocent student-consumer who is presently being
forced to maintain in employment an academic whose services
he does not wish. It would be the *non-innocent* ruling class
which is being so forced. If the ruling class theory is correct, aca-
demicians with views favorable to the ruling class have nothing
to gain from academic freedom. They will be retained in their
jobs in any case. It is the academic with views that are *not*
amenable to the ruling class, and he alone, who benefits. He
gains from academic freedom because it prevents *ruling class*

---

[1]See G. William Domhoff, *The Higher Circles* (New York: Random
House, 1970).

employers from dismissing him on ideological or other nonformalistic grounds.

Academic freedom, as such, can be looked upon as a fraud and theft, because it denies individuals the right of free and voluntary contracts. But that a "bad" means can also be used for good ends should occasion no surprise.

9
THE ADVERTISER

Advertising has long had a "bad press." The case against it is detailed and seemingly compelling. It is claimed that advertising entices people, forcing them to buy products they would otherwise not buy. It preys on the fears and psychological weaknesses of people. It is misleading, with its justaposition of a beautiful woman and a commercial product, implying that she is somehow part of the deal. It is foolish, what with its contests, marching bands, and jingles. It is an insult to our intelligence.

The argument is usually capped with an appeal to our selfish natures—advertising is very costly. A minute of prime television time or a full-page adverstisement in a popular magazine or newspaper can run into thousands of dollars. The advertising industry as a whole is a multibillion dollar industry. If we banned advertising, it is alleged, all of this money could be saved. The money could then be used to improve the product, or lower its price, or both. The advertising industry could be replaced with a governmental board which would present objective descriptions and ratings. Instead of sexy misleading jingles, we would have product descriptions, perhaps summarized by a grade level of "Grade A," "Grade B," etc. In any case, the advertisers, who are

nonproductive and essentially parasitical, would be put out of business.

There is much that is wrong with this view of advertising, but it is not without its historical precedents. In fact, it is only the most recent in a long line of arguments purporting to show that one or another industry is parasitical and unproductive. The physiocrats, a school of economic thought in mid-eighteenth century France, thought all industries except farming, fishing, and hunting were wasteful. They reasoned that anything not connected with the soil was sterile, and dependent and parasitical upon the soil-based industries. Other economists have distinguished between goods, which were considered productive, and services, which were not. Still others have held that all goods but only some services were productive. For example, it has been denied that monetary services such as financial intermediation, brokerage, banking, and speculation have any value. It is easy, nowadays, to see the limitations of these theories. A good need not come directly from the soil to be productive, nor need a service be "tangible," such as medical care, to be productive. We know that brokers bring people together at lower costs than they could manage on their own. We know that the nontangible product of the insurance industry provides for the pooling and consequent lessening of risks. But even in these sophisticated times the advertising industry enjoys a widespread reputation as a parasite.

How strong is the case? First, it seems clear that advertising does not lure or force people to buy what they would not otherwise buy. Advertising attempts to persuade people—perhaps in ways some members of the community find objectionable. But it does not and cannot *coerce*. (Fraudulent advertising is logically equivalent to theft, and is not to be confused with advertising *per se*. If the seller advertises wheat but delivers rocks, he has actually stolen the money price of "wheat.")

Subliminal advertising, if it exists, would be considered coercive. But it cannot be claimed that ordinary advertising is coercive without completely obliterating the distinction between coercion and persuasion.

Second, advertising does have an informational content. This is conceded even by its most fervent detractors, although they think that the government could do a better job. But governmental action in the field of advertising is no less advertising just because it is government advertising. If anything, there are more problems which are harder to deal with in "government issued" advertisements. Unencumbered by the usual necessity to make profits by pleasing consumers, when the government gets out of hand, there is very little that can be done. Governmental advertising for United States War Bonds or the military draft are but two examples that come to mind.

Third, the importance of advertising in helping new companies, and thus encouraging competition, should not be underestimated. If advertising were prohibited, the large established companies would have a powerful advantage in the market. Even with things as they are, older firms are more likely to monopolize a given industry than newer ones. Advertising, by giving a comparative advantage to newcomers, lessens the degree of concentration in the economy.

Finally, much if not all of the advertising that violates community standards of intelligence and decency can be traced to and blamed on governmental edicts in other areas. For example, the government[1] does not allow airlines to compete with one another in trivial areas. Their advertising campaigns bombard us with "news" about early bird specials, new decor, the number of seats in an aisle, airplanes named after stewardesses, etc. ("I'm Marybeth. Fly me to Miami"). If airlines were free to compete with respect to price, the passengers might be spared this constant reiteration about nonessential affectations.

The same is true for banks. Banks are limited in the amount of interest they can pay to depositors (zero percent to demand depositors, 5½ percent–7½ percent to time depositors, as of this date). They compete, therefore, with each other as to which can give the best kitchen utensils, radios, etc., as lures for new depositors. (Note that since they can charge as much as the market will bear for loans, they spend far less advertising money to try to convince anyone to *borrow* money from them.) The true

---

[1]For the view that it was not the government that initiated controls of this type in an effort to regulate business in the public interest, but rather business in an effort to control the competition of newcomers, see Gabriel Kolko, *Triumph of Conservatism* (New York: Quadrangle, 1967).

blame for advertisements of this kind belongs not to the advertising industry, but to the government.

These four arguments, when taken together, constitute a valid defense against the critics of advertising. Yet they do not strike at the heart of the matter. For they ignore the main fallacy of the critics—the assumption that deep down, there is a distinction to be made between motivational advertising and informational advertising, that motivational advertising is "bad" in various ways while informational advertising is "good." The truth is, however, that exposing people to information and motivating them are so inextricably bound up together that it makes little sense to even distinguish between them.

For a better perspective, consider several examples where it is not *they* who are trying to impart information and motivation to *us*, but *we* who are trying to impart information and motivation to *them*. Most of *us*, for instance, have had the experience of being interviewed for a new position. How do we prepare? We commence by writing an advertising brochure about ourselves. (This document is sometimes called a "resume" by those anxious to obfuscate and to hide the fact that each of us is, at almost all times, an advertiser.) In this advertising brochure we put the facts of our employment life as they pertain to the prospective job. And in splendid advertising tradition, we try to make these facts appear as flattering as possible. We hire a professional typist to help "entice" an employer into hiring us, and we have the brochure printed on fine paper in order to "create an impression," as a good advertiser should.

Strictly speaking, we are only providing information on the brochure. It is "merely" informational advertising on the face of it, but the attempt to present the information in a favorable light involves us, willy nilly, in motivational advertising.

During the interview, we continue to advertise. We "package" ourselves as best we can. Even though we might not do so every day, at the job interview we will give special attention to grooming effects.

Even when not engaged in job-hunting, we advertise, by constantly trying to portray ourselves in a good light. Even unconsciously we try to package ourselves well. From the very cradle parents are busy advertising us or laying the groundwork for future advertising. How else can we explain those ballet, violin and piano lessons and visits to the orthodontist or skin doctor?

The "Jewish mother," with her constant exhortations about good posture and good eating habits ("Eat, eat, children are starving in Europe and you're not eating"), is the great unsung heroine of the advertising business. And the Jewish mother's bragging about her children? Just more advertising.

As we grow up we carry on the fine traditions of advertising. We wear clothing that flatters our figures. We diet, or try to. At least part of our expenditures on education, psychiatry, hair grooming, and clothing can only be understood as advertising expenditures. Later on we purchase cars, houses, recreation, in large part as advertisements for ourselves. Incidentally, the greater expenditures (as a percentage of income) on "luxury" items such as clothing and cars, made by groups who are discriminated against, such as women and blacks, can be explained by advertising.[2] They feel they must engage in greater advertising expenses in order to counteract the discrimination. The rest need not invest so heavily in advertising because *we* are *in*.

Even members of the radical left, who are among the bitterest critics of advertising, engage in advertising themselves. (This should not be surprising, since we are defining advertising in its proper but broad sense of creative and interesting packaging.) Usually whenever the radical left has access to a bulletin board, the messages placed on it are at first uniformly small, neat, and similarly printed. After a while, in order to attract attention, some of the messages are printed in different colors, and on different-size placards. Eventually, in the competition to attract attention, larger and larger placards are used, with bolder printing, coloring, and illustrations. In their attempt to spread information, they are led "as if by an invisible hand" to engage in motivational advertising. The reason radicals write messages

---

[2]This point has been made by Professor Benjamin Klein of the department of economics, University of California, Los Angeles.

such as, "OFF THE PIG" or "FUCK THE STATE" on walls
or buildings in big red letters, is not entirely out of a desire to
shock. It is also out of a desire to impart the revolutionary message, by first attracting attention to it. If it is not read, however
informational it may be, it will impart no information. But as
much can be said for the typical soap opera advertisement.

Anyone who has ever been called upon to give a speech
where there was a distinct possibility of putting the audience to
sleep will understand the difficulty of distinguishing between
imparting information and packaging a speech. Surely, no more
boring a speech can be imagined than a lecture on economics.
The public speaker or teacher will engage in certain practices,
such as maintaining eye contact, telling jokes, or posing rhetor-
ical questions. These are sometimes known as public speaking
techniques. A more appropriate term would be "advertising
techniques"—packaging the product well, making it appear
interesting, highlighting the talk, bringing points into focus, and
capturing the attention of the audience. These advertising techniques have about as much to do with the subject of the talk as
bicycling has to do with Coca-Cola, as deep throaty, sexy female
voices have to do with shaving cream, or as the sporting events
of "the more than one beer men" have to do with beer. That is
not the point. The point is that if one hopes to get information
across—even to people who are well-motivated, such as the stu-
dent in the economics class who has to stay awake to receive a
good grade—one must engage in advertising techniques. If this
is important when dealing with people who are well-motivated,
imagine how much more important it is to "advertise" information when your "audience" is not well-motivated. Television
advertising should be interpreted at least as favorably, if not
more so, than the advertising engaged in by public speakers.
They are both attempts to impart information by making that
information interesting and attractive. But the television ad faces
the additional burden of keeping the viewer away from his
refrigerator. If all content which was not strictly informational
was banned, we would have to prevent speakers and teachers
from even *attempting* to be interesting. They would not be

allowed to tell jokes, maintain eye contact, or discuss questions with the audience. These techniques are above and beyond the strict imparting of information. Like television advertising gimmicks, they are attempts to "waylay the audience."

Is it *possible* to ban motivational advertising while allowing informational advertising? No. Information can be presented well or badly (i.e., in such a way as to bore and alienate the audience, or charm and amuse it), but it must be "packaged" or "presented" in *some* way. For example, imagine that a magic carpet was invented, and it was decided that information about it was to be given out (the flying speed, cruising range, upkeep costs, how to roll it up and store it while not in use, etc.), but the presentation was to be purely informational. Anything which even hinted at "promotion" of the carpet would be banned. Given this condition, a regular television announcer, with his good looks, forcefulness and self-confidence, could not present the information. His personality might promote the carpet. Nor could there be music in the background. It might seem "inspirational." The carpet certainly could not be shown "in action," that is, with an attractive woman on it. We could not risk fooling people into believing that if they bought the carpet they would get a copy of the inspirational music or of the inspirational woman.

If we could not use a professional announcer, could we use a nonprofessional one, or just an ordinary man off the street? We could not. Some advertising companies with their low cunning are already using testimonials from the "man-in-the-street" with great success, proving that this procedure has a *motivational* content.

If the information cannot be read, can it be printed? But what kind of typeface should be used? Certainly not a style that would induce someone to—horrors!—*buy* the flying carpet. It would have to be an almost indecipherable typeface so that people could hardly read it. Otherwise, at a low enough price, many people would be led down the garden path into making a purchase. The whole message would have to be presented in a purposely inferior manner so as not to attract any attention to itself.

Clearly, there is no way to separate the "package" from what it contains. There is no way to present "pure" information. To believe that the presentation of information without motivation is foolishness of the highest degree.

The objection that advertising adds to the cost of the product is an objection that has not been clearly thought out. Would the critics object because wrapping a product adds to the cost? Or transporting it? They would not. It is understood that these additional costs are necessarily incurred if the product is to be made available to the consumer. But the same is true of advertising! Suppose the magic carpet previously mentioned costs $950 to manufacture, $10 to wrap it, and $40 for transportation. If customers want to take advantage of the wrapping and delivery services, they must pay the full $1,000. But they have the choice of picking up a wrapped carpet at $960, an unwrapped one for $950, or an unwrapped one delivered to their homes for $990.

So is it with advertising costs. If it costs $100 to advertise the carpet, the customers have a choice between the advertised brand for $1,100 and an unadvertised brand (which presumably, they could find if they searched long enough) for $1,000. If a substantial number of consumers were willing to find unadvertised brands or outlets, manufacturers would be foolish to advertise. However, some consumers may not be so enterprising or energetic in shopping for unadvertised brands at cheaper prices. This would give the manufacturer the incentive to advertise, and the costs of the advertisements would be added to the purchase price. It is true, therefore, that advertising would add to the cost of the product. But then it is true that advertising is necessary in order to bring the product to the people. If some refused to buy unwrapped, undelivered magic carpets, but *would* buy wrapped, delivered ones, could it be said that wrapping costs and delivery costs were added to the total costs *unnecessarily*? Decidedly not. In the same manner, advertising does not add unnecessarily to the costs of the product.

What of a governmental ratings board for advertising? Before giving the government still another task, because of alleged "imperfections" in the market, consider the dismal record of the government to date. The graft and corruption unearthed by Ralph Nader and his associates should give pause for thought. Regulation agency after regulation agency, from ICC and CAB to FTC, FPC, and others, have been shown to be regulating industry not for the benefit of the consumer, but for the benefit of the industry as against the consumer. And this is not just an accident. There is a reason for it.

Each of us is a purchaser of literally thousands of items, but producers of only one. Our ability to influence regulatory legislation passed by the state is, therefore, much more concentrated as producers than as consumers. Government agencies, accordingly, tend to regulate in favor of the producing industry rather than the mass of consumers. In fact, government regulatory agencies tend to be set up by the very industries they are to regulate. Milton Friedman, in the chapter entitled "Occupational Licensure" in *Capitalism and Freedom*,[3] brilliantly demonstrates the dismal record of governmental rating agencies in the medical field. There is no reason to assume that a rating agency in advertising would be any different. Rather, it would not be surprising if the calls for governmentally regulated "objective," "informational" advertising were begun by the larger, established, advertising firms as a way of slowing down the rising competition from smaller firms and newcomers.

But the strongest argument against governmental regulation of advertising is not the empirical one showing its dismal record to date, strong though that may be. The strongest argument is the logical one. The reasoning employed by those who want governmental regulation contains a self-contradiction. On the one hand they assert that the American people are unalterably gullible. They must be protected because, left to their own devices, they become victims. They can be made to think, for

---

[3]Milton Friedman, *Capitalism and Freedom* (Chicago: University of Chicago Press, 1962).

example, that if they use a certain brand of aftershave lotion, they will end up with the girl in the ad. On the other hand, the argument assumes that the boobs are smart enough to pick political leaders capable of regulating these sirens. This is impossible.

In any case, if the public is sufficiently enamored of "objective" information on consumer products, it can avail itself of the services of firms and organizations such as *Consumer Reports*, *Good Housekeeping*, the Better Business Bureau, commercial testing laboratories, and other private-enterprise certification agencies. The free market is flexible. It can provide this kind of service too. (But the inability to separate motivational and informational advertising still holds. When *Consumer Reports* states that Zilch Flakes are the best flakes to buy, it is necessarily motivating people to "buy Zilch" over and above other flakes. It cannot provide information without providing *any* motivation to do anything.)

Advertising can be defended only when it occurs on the free market. In the case of government or government-aided big business advertising, none of the free-market defenses hold. Here, people are forced to pay for the advertising whether they choose to buy the product or not. When the government advertises, it is with tax money collected on an involuntary basis. The advertising in which the government engages is highly motivational ("Uncle Sam Wants You") and not infrequently fraudulent. It is strange that government advertising has been so completely ignored, even by the most vociferous critics of advertising. Imagine what would ensue if a private businessman were to engage in fraudulent advertising on even 1 percent of the scale committed by Franklin Roosevelt, Lyndon Johnson, or Richard Nixon, who campaigned on advertised peace planks, and yet involved the country in foreign wars. How can we entrust punishment of fraudulent advertising to the worst fraudulent advertisers of all time—the government?

Finally, advertising must be defended by those who believe in freedom of speech—for that is all advertising is. It is all too easy to defend the right to speak of those whose speech we favor

in any case. But if the rights of free speech are to mean anything at all, those who are not in public favor must be
defended. Libertarians anxiously await a defense by the American Civil Liberties Union of the free speech rights of advertisers.
This organization was ominously quiet during the banning of
cigarette commercials from television.

10

THE PERSON WHO YELLS "FIRE!" IN A CROWDED THEATER

In a case against free speech, the "fire!" screamer is Exhibit A. Even those who argue in defense of civil liberties and the right of free speech stipulate that these rights do not include the right to yell "fire!" in a crowded theater. This is the one case where all parties seem to agree that the right to free speech is not as important as other rights.

But to override the right of free speech, for any reason, is a dangerous precedent, and never necessary. Certainly it is not necessary in the case of the person who yells "fire!" The rights of theater patrons can be protected without legally prohibiting free speech. For example, theater owners could contract with their customers not to yell "fire!" (unless, of course, there is a fire in the theater). The contract might take the form of an agreement, in small print, on the back of a theater ticket or a large message on wall posters placed throughout the theater, prohibiting any disturbance of the entertainment or singling out the shouting of the word, "fire!" But however the prohibition appeared, the contract would effectively put an end to the supposed conflict between the right of free speech and other rights. For the person who yelled "fire!" would then simply be violating

"Oh, miss, would you happen to know the Spanish word for 'Fire'?"

a contract and could be dealt with accordingly. The situation would be entirely analogous to that of someone under contract to sing at a concert, but who refuses to sing, and instead lectures on economics. What is involved in both cases is not the right of free speech, but the obligation to honor a contract. Why look at the prohibition in this way? There are several important reasons.

First, the market would be much more effective in removing threats to the public health and safety—such as the one posed by the "fire!" screamer—than an all-encompassing governmental prohibition. A market contract system would work more efficiently because theater entrepreneurs would be in competition with each other with regard to the efficiency with which they prevented outbursts disruptive to the audience. Thus, they would have a great incentive to diminish the number and severity of such outburts. The government, on the other hand, offers no incentive. No one *automatically* loses money when the government fails to maintain order in a theater.

A second reason we can expect greater success from the market than from the government is that the market is, by its very nature, more flexible. The government can only make one all-embracing rule, with at best, one or two exceptions. The market does not have such restrictions. The flexibility and complexity of the market are limited only by the inventiveness of the actors in it.

Third, the government system of protection against yelling "fire!"—outright prohibition—violates the rights of perhaps one of the most oppressed minorities: the sadists and the masochists. What of the rights of the sadists who enjoy yelling "fire!" in a crowded theater, and then watching the crowd tear itself to pieces in the resultant mad rush for the exits? What of the masochists who relish the thought of having "fire!" yelled at them while in the confines of a crowded theater with the same mad but "exhilarating" crush at the door? Under the government system of outright prohibition, these people are denied what may be their most fervent wish—their chance to go out in a blaze of glory. In the flexible market system, however, where there is a demand for a service, a supply will soon arise. Where there is an unfulfilled demand for sado-masochists screaming "fire!" and then watching the frantic crushes, entrepreneurs will rise to the occasion and provide the requisite service.

Such musings will undoubtedly strike the "straights" on the sado-masochistic question as just so much idle talk. But that is only to be expected. No ruling class ever viewed the plight of their downtrodden with anything but contempt and scorn. Nonaggressing adult sado-masochists have just as much right to their mutually agreeable practices as anyone else. To dismiss the rights of sado-masochists as not being worthy of consideration provides evidence of the fascistic habits of thought to which most "straights" have succumbed. Sado-masochists should be free to indulge in their nonaggressive practices. The public, after all, need not attend any theater which clearly advertises that "unplanned disruptions" will be permitted. Sado-masochists, for their part, would still have to curb their enthusiasm when patronizing "straight" theaters.

Finally, unless the prohibition against yelling "fire!" in a crowded theater stems from a private contract, the right of free speech will be in conflict with what is held in very high esteem—namely the rights of people not to have their show interrupted and themselves crushed at the exits.

Freedom of speech is at best a weak reed. It is always in danger of being suppressed. Our hold on it is sometimes very tenuous indeed. Therefore, anything which tends to weaken it even further must be opposed. There is hardly a scare tactic better designed to destroy freedom of speech than the creation of a false conflict between the right to speak freely and other rights held in vastly higher esteem. Yet this is precisely what the usual interpretation of yelling "fire!" accomplishes. If "exceptions" to the right of free speech are granted, our tenuous hold on the right of free speech is weakened. There are *no* legitimate exceptions to the right of free speech. There are *no* cases in which the right of free speech is in conflict with any other right we hold dear.

Therefore, the person who yells "fire!" in a crowded theater can be considered a hero. He forces a consideration of what is involved and what needs to be done to protect a precious right that is endangered.

IV. OUTLAW

11

THE GYPSY CAB DRIVER

The taxi business in the United States usually works to the detriment of the poor and minority groups in two ways—as consumers and as producers. As consumers, their plight is well demonstrated by ethnic "taxicab jokes," and by the subterfuge and embarrassment blacks undergo in order to get a cab, which they are frequently unable to do. The reasons are not difficult to fathom. Taxi rates are set by law and are invariant, regardless of the destination of the trip. However, some destinations are more dangerous than others, and drivers are reluctant to service these areas which are usually the home neighborhoods of the poor and the minorities. So when given a choice, cab drivers are likely to select customers on the basis of their economic status or skin color.

It is important to realize that given the differential crime rates, it is *solely* government control of taxi rates that engenders this situation. In the absence of such controls, rates to unsafe areas could be set so as to compensate cab drivers for the greater risks involved. If this were done, blacks would have to pay more than whites for a cab, if not in the form of higher payments on the meter, perhaps in the form of older or lower quality cabs. But at least they would be able to secure the services of a taxi if they

"Xerox 57 3/8—up 1/8, Texas Instrument 92—up 2, Sun Oil preferred 31—down a quarter, New York City Taxi Medallions $96,090—up $245.00."

so desired. Under the present system, they do not even have the choice.

The inability to obtain a cab is not a small inconvenience to the poor black consumer, although many of the white middle class might think otherwise. Public transportation (bus, trolley, and train) plans and routes were designed and constructed 50 to 75 years ago. In those years transportation lines were usually owned by *private* concerns who were dependent on their customers for their profits and success. They were designed specifically to meet customer needs. In many cases, these transport lines are unsuitable for the needs of the present-day community. (Transit lines today are publicly owned and, therefore, lack the incentive to tailor them to the needs of the customer. If customers refuse to patronize a transit corridor, and that corridor becomes unprofitable, the public authority simply makes up the difference out of general tax revenues.) Consequently, city dwellers must choose between a fast ride home by taxi, and a long, indirect, and halting ride via public transit. This is especially true for the poor and minority groups who lack the political power to influence public transit authorities or decisions concerning the construction of new lines.

Restricted access to cabs in areas where public transportation is inadequate is often more than inconvenient. When health is involved, for example, the cab is an excellent and cheap substitute for an ambulance. But in poor neighborhoods which are inadequately served by public transportation, and whose residents cannot afford private cars, it is usually difficult to find a taxi.

Under the present system, the poor also suffer as producers. In New York City, for example, the government requires all cabs to be licensed. The licenses—medallions—are strictly limited in number—so much so, that they have been sold for as much as $30,000. The price varies, depending on whether the medallion is for an individual cab or part of a fleet. This effectively bars the poor from entering the field as owners. What would have happened to the Horatio Alger hero if he had needed $30,000 *before* he could enter the shoe-shine or newspaper delivery business?

Some years ago, in response to the limitations placed upon them both as consumers and as producers, the poor and minority group members began to enter the taxi industry in a time honored American tradition dating back to the Revolutionary War of 1776—disobedience of the law. They simply had their used cars outfitted with meters, special lights and signs, and declared them to be cabs. In these "gypsy" cabs, they cruised the streets of the ghetto areas which were shunned by medallioned taxi drivers, and began to earn an honest, albeit illegal living. Their initial success in avoiding punishment under the existing laws was probably due to two factors: police fear of "unrest" in the ghetto if these cabs were harassed, and the fact that the gypsies worked only within the ghetto, and, therefore, did not take business from the medallioned cabs.

These idyllic times, however, were not to last. Gypsy cab drivers, perhaps emboldened by their success in the ghetto, began to venture outside. If the medallioned taxi drivers had looked upon the gypsies with suspicion before, they now exhibited outright hostility toward them. And with good reason. At this time, the taxi lobby in New York succeeded in pressuring the City Council to enact a bill allowing an increase in taxi fares. Patronage dropped precipitously and the immediate effect was a sharp decrease in the income of medallioned taxi drivers. It became obvious that many of their former riders were using gypsy cabs. At this juncture irate medallioned taxi drivers began to attack and burn gypsy cabs, and they retaliated in kind. After a few violent weeks, a compromise was reached. Yellow, the traditional color of taxicabs, was to be reserved for medallioned cabs. The gypsies would have to use another color. A tentative plan for licensing gypsy cabs was also discussed.

What of the future of the taxi industry in New York City? If the dominant "liberal consensus" politics holds sway, as it usually does in questions of this kind, some compromise with the gypsies will be reached and they will be brought under the rule of the taxi commission. Perhaps they will be granted a restricted license, out of deference to the yellow cabs. If so, the system will remain the same as it is at present —a situation which resembles a gang of robbers allowing a few new members to join. But the robbery will not be halted, nor the victims substantially helped. Suppose, according to one plan, 5,000 new licenses are created. This may help in a minor way in that there will be extra cabs potentially available for blacks. Thus, although blacks will still be second-class citizens, they may have a slightly easier time finding a cab. But, paradoxically, this concession to the greater need for cabs will stifle future demands for improvements. It will enable the taxi commission to pose as the liberal and bountiful grantor of taxi medallions based on its act of "generosity" in licensing gypsy cabs (even though it has not granted a single extra medallion since 1939).

As producers and entrepreneurs, the position of the poor may improve somewhat, for an additional 5,000 licenses may result in a decreased purchase price of a medallion. However, there is a possibility that the purchase price will rise after the extra 5,000 licenses are granted. For the great uncertainty presently keeping down the value of a medallion may well end. If it does, the value of medallions will remain high, and the position of the poor will not have improved at all.

No! A proper solution to the taxicab crisis is not to co-opt the movement of gypsy cab drivers by the offer to take them into the system, but rather to destroy the system of restrictive cab licenses.

In terms of the everyday workings of the market, it would mean that *any* qualified driver with a valid chauffeur's license could use *any* vehicle which has passed the certification examination to pick up and deliver fares to *any* street of their mutual choosing, for *any* mutually agreeable price. The market for taxicabs in New York City would thus work in much the same way that rickshaws work in Hong Kong. Or, to take a less exotic example, the taxicab market would work in much the way that the babysitter market operates—completely dependent upon mutual agreement and consent between the contracting parties.

The taxi problems encountered by the poor and minority group members would be quickly resolved. Residents in high crime areas could then offer the cab drivers a premium. Though it is deplorable that they will be forced to pay this premium, they would no longer be second-class citizens insofar as obtaining a cab was concerned. The only real and lasting solution to this problem, however, is a reduction in the high crime rate in ghetto areas, which would be responsible for the extra charges. For the present, however, the people living in these areas must not be prohibited from taking the necessary steps to obtain adequate cab service.

Poor people would benefit as producers, as they set up their own businesses. They would, of course, have to assume ownership of a car, but the artificial and insurmountable $30,000 barrier would be removed.

There are, however, objections that will be raised to a free market in taxicabs:

(1) "A free market would lead to chaos and anarchy if medallions were eliminated. Taxis would flood the city and weaken the capacity of any cab driver to earn a living. So drivers would leave the industry in droves, and there would be far fewer taxis available than needed. Without medallions to regulate the number of taxis, the public would be caught between two unsatisfactory alternatives."

The answer is that even if there were an initial rush into the industry, and the market was glutted, only *some* drivers would leave the field. The number of cabs, therefore, would not swing erratically from an horrendous oversupply, to none at all, and back again. Moreover, the drivers who would tend to leave the industry would be the inefficient ones whose earnings were low or those with better alternatives in other industries. By leaving they would allow the earnings of those who remained to rise, and thus stabilize the field. One does not, after all, gain any insurance against the possibility of too many or too few lawyers, doctors, or shoe-shine boys by fixing an arbitrary upper limit to the number of people who can enter these occupations. We depend upon the forces of supply and demand. When there are too many workers in a field, the relative salaries decrease, and some will be encouraged to enter other occupations; if too few, wages and new occupants increase.

(2) The argument that licensing protects the riding public is one of the most disingenuous arguments for taxi medallions. It is the same one used by psychiatrists, who strive to "protect" us

from encounter groups and others who make inroads in their incomes, by lily white unionists who "protect" the public by keeping qualified blacks out, and by doctors who "protect" us by refusing to grant medical licenses to qualified foreign doctors. Few people are fooled by these arguments today. Surely the special chauffeur's license test and car inspections can insure the quality of drivers and cars.

(3) "The medallion would have no value if there were an unlimited amount of taxis. This would be unfair to all those who have invested thousands of dollars in the purchase of their medallions."

Some light can be shed on this argument by considering a short fable:

A warlord granted permission to a group of highwaymen to rob all passersby. For this right, the warlord charged the highwaymen a fee of $2,500. And then the people overthrew the system.

Who should bear the cost of what turned out to be an unprofitable investment on the part of the highwaymen? If the choice was limited to the warlord and the robbers, we might say, "A plague on both your houses." If we had to choose between them, we might root for the highwaymen, on the grounds that they were less of a threat than the warlord, and perhaps had made the original payment out of monies honestly earned. But in no case would we countenance a plan whereby the long suffering highway travelers were forced to pay off the highwaymen for having lost the privilege of robbing them!

In the same way, the argument should not be accepted that the long suffering taxi riding *public* should compensate owners for valueless medallions already purchased. If it ever came to a showdown between medallion owners and medallion grantors (politicians), the public should perhaps favor the owners, on the grounds that they pose less of a danger to them and perhaps had originally paid for their medallions with money honestly earned. It is the politicians' *personal* funds, or the funds of their estates which should be used to pay off the medallion owners. A warlord is a warlord. Payment out of public funds would only

12

THE TICKET SCALPER

W ebster's dictionary defines "scalper" as one who "buys and sells in order to make quick profits," and "scalping" as "cheating, defeating, and robbing." The latter definition is the one used by the public in its hostility toward "ticket scalpers."

The reason for this condemnation is easy to discern. Imagine a theatergoer or sports fan on the eve of the big event, arriving and finding, much to his consternation, that he must pay $50 for a $10 seat. He thinks that these outrageous prices are charged by "scalpers," who purchase tickets at normal prices and then deliberately withhold them until people are so desperate that they were willing to pay any asking price. An economic analysis, however, will show that the condemnation of the ticket scalper is unjust.

Why does scalping exist? A *sine qua non* of scalping, a necessary condition for its existence, is a fixed, invariable supply of tickets. If the supply could increase with increased demand, the scalper would be totally displaced. Why would anyone patronize a scalper when he could purchase additional tickets from the theater at the printed list price?

A second necessary condition is the appearance on the ticket of a list price. If a stipulated price did not appear on the ticket, scalping, by definition, could not occur. Consider shares of stock bought and sold on the New York Stock Exchange on which there is no printed price. No matter how many are bought, how long they are held, or how high the price at which they are resold—they cannot be "scalped."

Why do theaters and ballparks print ticket prices? Why not allow them to be sold at whatever price the market will bring, the way wheat is sold in the Chicago futures market or shares of stock in the stock market? If they were, scalping would be eliminated. Perhaps the public looks upon printed prices on tickets as a great convenience; perhaps it helps people to budget, plan vacations, etc. Whatever the reason, the public must prefer prices to be stipulated. If it did not, managers and producers would find it in their interest not to do so. Thus the second necessary condition for scalping exists by popular demand.

The third condition which must be present is that the ticket price chosen by management be lower than the "market clearing price" (the price at which the number of tickets people are willing to buy is just equal to the number of seats available).

Stipulated prices *lower* than the market clearing price are open invitations to ticket scalping. For at the lower price there are more customers willing to buy tickets than there are tickets available. This imbalance sets in motion forces which tend to correct it. Would-be purchasers begin to try harder to obtain tickets. Some of them become willing to pay more than the price printed on the ticket. Prices rise, and the original imbalance is corrected as these higher prices cause a drop in demand.

Why do theater or ballpark managers set their ticket prices below the market clearing price? For one thing, lower prices invite a large audience. Long lines of people waiting to enter a theater or ballpark constitutes free publicity. In other words, management forgoes higher prices in order to save money it might have had to spend on advertising. In addition, managers are loath to raise ticket prices—even though they would have little difficulty selling them for a big event or special movie—for

"Well, even if he is a scalper I admire his spunk."

fear of a backlash. Many people feel that there is a "fair" price for a movie ticket, and managers are responsive to this feeling. Thus, even though they might be able to charge higher than usual prices for a movie like "The Godfather," they choose not to. They know many people will refuse to patronize the theater at a later time, feeling that the management "took advantage" of the public during the showing of this very popular movie. There are several other motivations, less compelling, for keeping prices fixed at below equilibrium levels. Taken together they ensure that this pricing policy—the third condition necessary for scalping—will continue.

In taking a closer look at the positive function fulfilled by the ticket scalper, it has been shown that when tickets are priced below the equilibrium level, there are more customers than tickets. The problem becomes one of rationing the few tickets among the many claimants. It is in the solution to this problem that the ticket scalper plays his role.

Suppose that during the baseball season the price of an average ticket is $5.00 and the ballpark is filled to its capacity of 20,000 for every game. However, for the "big game" at the end of the season, 30,000 people want tickets. How will the 20,000 tickets be distributed or rationed among the 30,000 people willing to buy them? Which 10,000 of the 30,000 hopefuls will have to forgo the game?

The two basic ways of rationing goods that are in short supply have been defined by economists as "price rationing" and "nonprice rationing." In price rationing, prices are allowed to rise. This, in our opinion is the only fair way to ration a commodity when demand exceeds supply. In the example above, the average price of a ticket may rise to $9.00 if that is the price at which there will be only 20,000 people ready and willing to buy the 20,000 tickets. The specific *procedure* through which this increase of $4.00 in the average price of a ticket takes place varies. Ticket speculators or "scalpers" might be permitted to buy all the tickets and resell them at $9.00 per ticket. Or, they might be permitted to buy 2,000 tickets, the other 18,000 being sold for the printed ticket price of $5.00. They might sell the 2,000 tickets for $45.00 each, and this would also result in an average price of $9.00 per ticket. Though the ticket scalpers would be blamed for the "outrageously high" prices, the price would really be the result of simple arithmetic. For if an average price of $9.00 is necessary to reduce the demand for tickets to the available 20,000, and if 18,000 of them are sold at $5.00 each, then the remaining 2,000 *must* be sold at $45.00.

In nonprice rationing, prices are not allowed to rise in order to decrease the demand to the level of the available supply. Instead, other techniques are employed to attain the same end. The management may distribute the tickets on a first-come, first-served basis. It may employ other types of favoritism in order to narrow down the market—nepotism (selling the tickets only to relatives or friends), racism (selling them to only certain racial groups), sexism (selling them only to males). Certain age groups may be singled out and all others barred, or perhaps war veterans or members of certain political parties may be given special privileges. All these nonprice rationing techniques are discriminatory and arbitrarily favor some groups over others.

Consider a typical first-come, first-served (FCFS) method, since this is the type of system most widely used and the one usually thought to be "fair." Though tickets are not scheduled to be sold until 10:00 a.m. of the day of the event, hopeful customers line up outside the box office long before. Some join the line at the crack of dawn; some even begin the night before. FCFS is thus discriminatory against those who find waiting in line particularly onerous, those who cannot take a day off from work to wait in line, or those who cannot afford to hire servants or chauffeurs to wait in line for them.

Does price rationing, and therefore, ticket scalping, favor the rich? An equivocal answer must be given. From one perspective, ticket scalping helps the lower and middle class, and hurts the rich. Assuming that the lowest income class includes more people who are unemployed or marginally employed, they have time and opportunity to wait in line. Even if employed, they do not lose as much as others when they take time off from work. For these people who have few options, ticket scalping provides employment and business opportunities. There is no other pursuit in which a poor person can begin his own business with so little capital. In the case stated above, all that is needed is $50.00 to buy ten $5.00 tickets. When and if these are resold at $45.00 each, a profit of $400.00 is gained.

Members of the middle class are helped as well, for these people are less likely to have time available for waiting in ticket lines. It is more costly for them (in terms of income lost) to take time off from work than for a member of the lower class. It is prudent for the member of the middle class to buy his ticket from the scalper for $45.00 rather than wait in line and lose far more, which he might have earned had he gone to work. In short, ticket scalping allows people in the lowest income brackets to serve as the paid agents of people in the middle class, who are too busy to wait in line for cheap tickets.

Rich people have servants who can wait in long lines for them and, therefore, do not need scalpers. In one case, however, the ticket scalper can help even the rich—when the scalper, who is a specialist, can do the job for less than it would cost the rich man to use a servant for the task. (It should occasion no surprise that ticket speculation can benefit *all* people. The market is not a jungle where people can only benefit at the expense of others. Voluntary trade is the paradigm case of mutually beneficial action.) If the scalper's profit margin is less than what it would cost the rich man to use a servant, he can buy the ticket directly from the scalper, cut out the middleman servant, and save the extra money.

From another perspective, however, price rationing and ticket scalping favor the rich, by ensuring that they will find it easier to purchase tickets at the high market price, while the rest of the public may find it difficult or impossible. However, this is the essence of a monetary economy and must be accepted as long as we wish to reap the benefits only such a system can provide.

In the chapter on the importer, a defense will be made of a monetary economy because it enables us to specialize and to benefit from the division of labor. Imagine the quality of life and the chances for survival if each of us was limited to what we could produce ourselves. The spectre is frightening. Our lives depend on trade with our fellows, and most if not all of the people presently living would perish if the monetary system fell.

The degree to which we do not permit money to ration goods, the degree to which we do not allow the rich to obtain a greater share of the goods of society in proportion to their monetary spending, is the degree to which we allow the monetary system to deteriorate. It is, of course, unfair to allow the rich to obtain a greater share of goods and services, to the degree that many of them amassed their fortunes not through the market but because of government aid. However, eliminating the monetary system in order to rid it of illicitly gathered fortunes would be like throwing out the baby with the bath water. The answer lies in directly confiscating the ill-gotten wealth.

When wealth is earned honestly, there is nothing inappropriate about being able to receive a greater share of goods and services, and it is essential to the preservation of the monetary system. The scalper, by facilitating the price rationing of tickets, is instrumental in assisting the rich in obtaining the rewards of their efforts.

13

THE DISHONEST COP

The hero of *Serpico*, a best selling book and movie, is a renegade, bearded, hippie cop who refuses to obey the unspoken code of policemen, "Don't turn against your fellow officers." As Serpico states, "The only oath I ever took was to enforce the law—and it didn't say against everybody except other cops."

The story traces Serpico's development, beginning with his boyhood ambition to be a good police officer. It reveals his initial naïveté about the corruption on the force, his solitary and unsuccessful attempts to interest the police brass in the situation, the contempt and hatred he experienced at the hands of his fellow officers, and his final disillusionment. Throughout, the assumption made about the "good guys" and the "bad guys" is evident. The good guys are Frank Serpico and one or two policemen who gave him limited aid in his quest for "justice" and punishment of the grafters. The bad guys were those cops on the take, and those who protect them from prosecution. It is precisely this view which should be questioned.

Serpico and Gambling

An envelope containing $300 plays an important part in the story of Serpico. It was delivered to him by a messenger from someone known only as "Jewish Max," a powerful gambler. After many attempts, Serpico was unable to interest any of his superior officers in the attempted bribe.

Why was "Jewish Max" attempting to bestow money and gifts on an unwilling Serpico? "Jewish Max," the purveyor of voluntary (gambling) services to consenting adults, was one of the intended victims of Serpico and other "honest" cops on the gambling squad! Their intention was to harass, chase, capture, and kidnap (jail) all those involved. The public is told that aggressive violent behavior on the part of the officers is necessary because gambling is against the law and it is their duty to uphold the law. But the most vicious Nazi thug in a concentration camp could claim this argument as a defense.

In another incident, a ghetto mother complained to Serpico that her son was being inducted into an illegal gambling operation. Serpico is asked to smash the operation. Now there can be little opposition to the attempt to protect a child from an activity that could be harmful to him. However, the disruption of an activity which is legitimate for adults, on the grounds that a child has become involved, is clearly objectionable. The solution in a case such as this lies in preventing the child from participation, not in the elimination of the activity. Sex, drinking, or driving should hardly be prohibited on the grounds that these activities are harmful or dangerous for children.

Serpico the Narc

Serpico is finally wounded while attempting to break into an apartment of a dope dealer, although his sworn duty is to *protect* the rights of citizens. The explanation, of course, is that selling narcotics is prohibited by law, and although he has sworn to protect the rights of individuals, Serpico has also sworn to uphold the law. In this instance, as elsewhere, when the two are contradictory, he chooses the latter. His participation on the narcotics squad itself demonstrates Serpico's overriding loyalty to the law.

But prohibiting the sale of narcotics invariably increases the purchase price, thereby making it difficult for addicts to obtain the drugs. Consequently, they must commit greater and greater crimes in order to obtain the necessary money. By prohibiting the sale of narcotics, the citizenry thus becomes endangered. To enforce that prohibition, as Serpico does, is to regard the protection of the law over that of the citizens.

Serpico and Cooping

Given that much of what the policeman is required to do is injurious to the general public, it follows that the less active the policeman is, the less injurious he will be to the public at large. The majority of policemen, perhaps sensing this, act so as to save the public from harm, i.e., they shun their duties.

Instead of being up and about, interfering with the rights of the people, many policemen choose the honorable way out—they coop. Cooping (sleeping in some out-of-the-way place while on duty) was a situation which enraged Serpico. In the finest tradition of the busybody who insists upon running other people's lives, Serpico insisted upon being out on the streets at all hours, stopping a prostitute here, ambushing a gambler there, harassing drug merchants everywhere.

It is, of course, impossible to deny that Serpico was also a force for good. He did, after all, hunt down rapists, muggers, robbers, thieves, murderers, and destroyers of the peace. Moreover, he carried out his duties in an enormously imaginative way. Disguised as a Hasidic Jew, a hippie, a slaughterhouse worker, a businessman, a drug addict, he prowled the city streets and unearthed its secrets as none of his fellow police officers— dressed in suits, ties, trenchcoats, black shoes, and white socks— could. But, the extent to which Serpico was able to achieve these accomplishments was the extent to which he was willing to step outside the realm of law and order.

Take the case of a young rapist. Serpico stopped a rape in progress, in spite of the opposition of his police partner, who objected to investigating the suspicious noises—on the grounds that they were taking place out of the area which he and Serpico were assigned to patrol. Oblivious to such specious reasoning, Serpico insisted upon an investigation. He was able to capture only one of the three rapists. When he brought him to the station house, Serpico was dismayed at the brutal (and ineffective) treatment to which the rapist was subjected. When the prisoner was about to be transferred to another location, Serpico brought him a cup of coffee, and talked kindly to him for several minutes. By using gentle persuasion he was able to unearth the names of the rapist's two accomplices.

Serpico then encountered the full pattern of bureaucratic red tape of the police department. He located the accomplices but, upon phoning his precinct commander to report on their whereabouts, was told that the detective assigned to the case was on vacation. The commanding officer insisted that Serpico *not* arrest the accomplices, even though he had them under surveillance from the phone booth. Serpico again disobeyed the *lawful* order from his commanding officer, and arrested the two men. (When he brought them to the station house he was told, by the angry commander, that he would not be given credit for the arrests—an appropriate ending to the story.)

It is instances such as this one which have made Serpico an all-time hero, and which account for the massive popularity of the book and movie. But this illustration also exposes the basic contradiction in Serpico's character. His attacks on prostitutes, gamblers, and drug sellers, all of whom were engaged in voluntary acts between mutually consenting adults, reveal his absolute devotion to the law. His boyhood dream of being a policeman, it will be remembered, was in terms of *upholding the law*. However, in the case of the rapist, Serpico does the good deed only because he is willing to violate the law. And in every case where his behavior can be considered heroic, the same principle of action is present.

In considering Serpico's battle against the other, "normal" policemen (the ones he considers corrupt), there are two types of cops. There are those who refuse to harass consenting adults engaging in voluntary though illegal activities, and who *accept* money from the individuals engaged in such activities; and there are those who *demand* money from these individuals for allowing them to engage in these activities.

In the first example, assuming the activities in question are legitimate, even though prohibited by law, it would seem perfectly proper to *accept* money for allowing them. The acceptance of money cannot be logically distinguished from the acceptance of a gift, and the mere acceptance of a gift is not illegitimate.

There are, however, some who take a contrary position by stating that exceptions cannot be made even in the case of ill-conceived laws; that "mere" individuals should not be free to pick and choose, but must simply obey the law. Allowing the law to be broken is necessarily evil, both in itself and because if taken as a precedent, it leads to chaos.

But it is difficult to countenance the notion that breaking the law is necessarily evil. Indeed, if the Nuremberg Trials have taught us anything, it is the diametric opposite of this view. The lesson of the Trials is that some laws are in and of themselves evil, and to obey them is wrong. It is equally difficult to understand the notion that selective law breaking establishes a precedent which ultimately leads to chaos. The only precedent such an action establishes is that *illegitimate* laws may be disobeyed. This does not imply chaos and arbitrary murder. It implies morality. Had such a precedent been firmly established at the time the Nazis came to power, concentration camp guards might have refused to obey *lawful* orders to murder hapless victims.

Finally, the notion that no "mere" individual should be free to pick and choose which law he will obey is nonsense. "Mere" individuals are all we have.

In conclusion, since lawbreaking can, on occasion, be legitimate, policemen who allow it are on occasion acting quite properly. Serpico's attacks upon such officers were, therefore, quite unwarranted.

Now consider the second kind of police officer condemned by Serpico—those who did not simply allow illegal activities, or accept money when offered, but *demanded* payment from citizens. The dictionary calls this extortion, "to draw from by force or compulsion; to wrest or wring from by physical force, violence, threats, *misuse of authority*, or by any illegal means; to exact money from, as conquerers extort contributions from the vanquished." Extortion is usually considered contemptible, and this evaluation is acceptable. However, does this imply approval of Serpico's attacks on the policemen involved in extortion? No, for Serpico's role was even worse than extortion! Consider four different ways a policeman may react to behavior which is illegal but perfectly moral. He may (1) ignore it, (2) accept money for ignoring it, (3) demand money for ignoring it (extortion), or (4) stop it.

Of the four possible reactions, the fourth is the least desirable, for it alone absolutely prohibits a moral activity—just because it happens to be illegal.

Had Serpico been a guard in a Nazi concentration camp, he would have felt it his duty to follow his orders to torture prisoners—as would all others who consider "law and order" the primary value. If he had consistently maintained his position, he would also have felt constrained to root out "corruption" in the camp by turning in those among his fellow officers who (1) refused to follow orders, (2) refused to follow orders and accepted payment from the prisoners, or (3) refused to follow orders and demanded payment (extortion). True, it is immoral to extort money from prisoners for not torturing them; but surely it is worse to not take their money—and instead, to obey orders and torture them.

V. Financial

14

THE (NONGOVERNMENT) COUNTERFEITER

The dictionary defines "counterfeit" as "forged; false; fabricated without right; made in imitation of something else with a view to defraud by passing the false copy for genuine or original." Thus, counterfeiting is a special case of fraud. In a general case of fraud, the "falseness" consists of passing some good or article off in return either for another good or for money. In the case of counterfeiting, what is passed off as genuine is not a commodity or an article, but money itself. This special case of fraud constitutes theft, just as fraud in general does. But with counterfeiting, there are certain complications.

The effects of counterfeiting depend entirely upon whether or not the counterfeit money is ever exposed as such. If it is, then the theft takes place in a rather straightforward way. If the falseness is discovered before the counterfeiter himself can pass it off to the first recipient, he will have been caught red-handed, and no counterfeiting will have taken place (point 1 in the diagram below). If the falseness is discovered after it has been given to the first recipient, but before he has had a chance to pass it on (point 2 in the diagram), the counterfeiting amounts to a theft from this first recipient. Mr. B has given up a genuine good or service for a piece of paper which is then discovered to be fraudulent and worthless. The piece of paper is destroyed, and the first recipient is left with nothing.

If the discovery is made after the first recipient has passed it off (unknowingly) to a second recipient, but before the second has had a chance to pass it along to a third, then this second recipient takes the loss (point 3).

Discovery of counterfeiting at point:

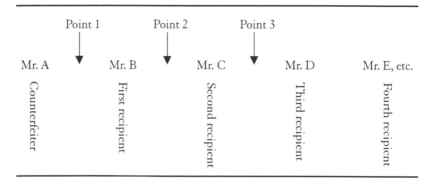

The second recipient loses because he has given the first recipient something of value, and has gotten nothing in return. If he can unearth the first recipient, the incidence of the loss would be complicated by the fact that the first recipient is innocent of any wrongdoing. The loss would probably have to be shared between the two recipients. Of course, if the original passer of the false money can be found and made to pay, no loss will have taken place, since in effect no counterfeiting will have taken place. But, if none of the previous passers can be found after the fact, the recipient who is discovered with the counterfeit money in his possession will bear the full loss, no matter how many times it has already been passed.

If the counterfeit money is never discovered, the situation is radically different. The losses due to counterfeiting are incurred, not by any one individual, but by the entire society, in a rather complicated way. The losses are not immediately apparent, for there is no *one* recipient who loses the total value of the commodity given up in return for the counterfeit money. But, it is

"I must say, young lady, it's refreshing to find someone acquainted with the evils of the Federal Reserve System, but where could I get gold or silver bullion at this time of night?"

easy to see that there are losses—for the counterfeiter has gained a value, without adding to the store of value of the rest of society. Since there are only so many goods in the society at any one time and the counterfeiter has gained some through fraud, there must be others who have lost out.

The way the loss is spread out though the society depends upon the rise in prices caused by the extra money (the counterfeited money) now in circulation. That prices *will* rise in response to the activities of the counterfeiters is a foregone conclusion, for counterfeiting increases the amount of money in circulation while the amount of goods and services remains the same. Prices will not rise all at once, nor will they rise smoothly and regularly. Rather, prices will rise in waves as does the water in a pool in response to a stone disturbing the equilibrium. They will first be driven up in the industry or area of which the first recipient of the counterfeit money is a member. Prices will be driven up because the counterfeit money spent in the industry is "extra"; that is, in the absence of the counterfeiting, it would not have been spent; therefore the first recipient benefits. He has received money which would not have been forthcoming but for the counterfeiting, and he is able to spend this extra money in an area where prices have not yet risen. The first recipient gains this incremental difference (though it may be substantial, it is in no way comparable to the counterfeiter's gain).

The second recipient also gains, as do all other recipients at the beginning of the ever-spreading ripple effect. For these people all receive the new money before prices have had a chance to be pushed up by the extra money put into circulation by counterfeiting. However, in time there will be a recipient of the imitation money who will just come out even. He will receive money at a time when it is still possible to spend part of it in an area which has not yet had a counterfeit-induced price rise. If he spends his money in an area which has not yet received a boost in prices, he will gain slightly from the inflation; if not, he will lose. On the average, people in this phase of the monetary expansion will be neither greatly benefited nor greatly harmed from the counterfeiting.

People receiving the counterfeit money *after* this stage bear the losses of the monetary expansion. Before they receive any extra money, prices will have risen. When the counterfeit money finally filters down to them they will be net losers. There are some groups, such as widows and retired people, who will always lose from counterfeiting, because during the spread of the counterfeit-induced inflation, their incomes are fixed.

If all this is true, how can the counterfeiter be considered a hero? Given that the main result of counterfeiting which is eventually discovered is to bilk the person caught "holding the bag," and that the main result of undiscovered counterfeiting is inflation which eventually harms many of us, it does indeed seem strange to call the counterfeiter a hero.

The justification for calling the common private counterfeiter heroic is that there is a *prior* counterfeiter in action and that the money falsified by the private counterfeiter is not really legitimate money; instead, it is itself counterfeit. It is one thing to say that counterfeiting *genuine* money amounts to theft; it is quite another thing to say that counterfeiting *counterfeit* money amounts to theft!

Perhaps an analogy will clarify this point. Taking someone's rightfully owned property is theft, and therefore unjustified. But no such proscription holds for taking the wrongfully owned (stolen) property of the thief. Indeed, such an activity need not even be called theft. In other words, an act which seems to be seemingly identical with theft is not illegitimate at all if the victim has no legitimate claim over the articles taken. If B steals something from A, and then C takes it away from B, we cannot hold C guilty of theft. (For the sake of simplicity, we can assume that the original owner, A, cannot be found by C.) A forced transfer of goods is illegitimate *only* if the original owner was the *rightful* owner; if he was not, there was nothing untoward about the transfer.

In like manner, we can see that it does not follow from the fact that counterfeiting genuine money is illegitimate that counterfeiting *counterfeit* money is illegitimate. If the claims can be substantiated that the counterfeiting of counterfeit money is not itself illegitimate; and that if the "original" money is indeed counterfeit, then it will have been demonstrated that the "private enterprise" counterfeiter is not guilty of wrongdoing, and can perhaps be considered heroic.

The claim that the counterfeiting of counterfeit money is not itself illegitimate is based on our understanding that such an activity is identical in form with stealing from a thief. The original dictionary definition of counterfeiting spoke of "fabricating without right," and of "passing the false copy for genuine or original." But if what is being copied is itself counterfeit, then the counterfeiter is not passing the false copy for genuine. He is only passing off (another) false copy. And if fabricating without right means passing something off as genuine, then our counterfeiter is not fabricating without right, for he is not in fact trying to pass something as genuine—he is only trying to pass his handiwork as a copy of a *counterfeit*.

The money which our counterfeiter is copying is itself counterfeit. It is made by a nonprivate counterfeiter—the government.

This is a serious charge, and is not made lightly. Unappetizing though it may be, the fact is that governments everywhere make counterfeits of real money—gold and silver. Virtually all governments then *forbid* the use of real money and allow only the use of the counterfeits they fabricate. This is equivalent to a private enterprise counterfeiter not only copying the money in circulation, but also preventing and prohibiting the circulation of the "legal" money.

Consider the monetary system before governments became deeply involved with it. Gold and silver (and paper certificates representing them) were the circulating medium. The government could not simply intrude on this system and impose its *fiat currency* (currency based upon the compulsion of emperors, kings, and presidents, not upon the voluntary decisions of the people). The people would not accept it as money, and would not voluntarily give up their hard earned possessions for such tokens. Instead, the government utilized gradualist methods in its quest to seize control of the monetary mechanism.

Under the gold standard, private minters converted gold bullion into coins. The weight of these coins was certified by the private minters, whose reputations for accuracy and probity were their main stock in trade. The first step of government was to seize monopoly control of the mints, proclaiming that coinage was the proper domain of the sovereign, and that private coiners could not be entrusted with such an important task. The government thus *nationalized* the mint.

The second stage was *debasement*. After affixing the picture of the monarch on the coin, to insure the weight and quality, the coins were "sweated" (stamped at a greater face weight than actual weight). It was in this way that government counterfeiting began.

The third step was the enactment of *legal tender laws*. These laws required that money be traded and counted at its official stamped value, and not at any other value, such as that based on weight. A coin stamped at 10 gold ounces could legally be used in payment of a debt of 10 gold ounces, even though the actual coin weighed only 8 gold ounces. The protests of the creditor were ignored by the sovereign's court system under the legal tender laws. The purpose of such laws was, of course, to establish the acceptability of money counterfeited by the government.

The government soon found that this was a small-time operation. There were limitations to the sweating of coins. However, even slowly replacing full-bodied coins (coins whose gold content equaled the stamped value) with token coins (coins which are intrinsically valueless as metals) would still not yield enough. Even if the government seized as much as 100 percent of the value of the coin, the value of all coins in total was limited. A course of action with much greater potential for counterfeiting was begun.

Step four was then introduced.[1] The government stopped simply replacing gold coins with token coins, and began creating tokens representing more gold than it possessed. Not the gold value of coins, nor of bullion, nor even the value of the gold in the ground, any longer limited the scope of government counterfeiting.

---

[1]We do not claim a strict, nonoverlapping temporal order for these stages. They are rather devices to clarify exposition.

With this innovation, government counterfeiting entered the fifth stage—the first "civilized" stage. Greenbacks, dollar bills, etc., could now be created seemingly without restraint. The printing presses were turned up to high speed, and government-counterfeit induced inflations began to take their place in the modern world.

With the sixth step, government spending received another "shot in the arm." Counterfeiting paper money, begun in the fifth stage, had been an "improvement" over counterfeiting coins, but the prospect of taking over banks and checkbook money offered an even greater improvement. Depending on the reserve requirements of the banks, the banking system could create a multiple monetary expansion, through the well-known "multiplier effect." In all expanding economies, paper money outstrips coins, and bank checking deposit money outstrips paper money. Taking over the banks, then (as well as the monopoly of coin and paper note issue), provided further scope for the counterfeiting plans of government.

Again under the guise that the free market could not be trusted, the government enacted legislation setting up the Central Bank, and later, the Federal Reserve System. The Central Bank was given a monopoly over paper money note issue, and the monetary tools (open market operations, setting the rediscount rate, and loans to banks) with which to keep the entire banking system in a harmonious state of counterfeiting.

The main argument used by the government was that the so-called "free" or "wildcat" banks, located mainly in inaccessible areas of the Midwest, were negligent in backing up their bank notes. This charge was true, in the main. But the reasons for it, which stem from the War of 1812, are illustrative. At the time of that war, New England banks were the soundest in the country. But New England was also the section of the country most opposed to the war. The central government thus had to borrow mainly from the Midwestern banks whose note issue far outstripped their gold stocks. (The government arrogated to itself the duty of maintaining the financial probity of the banks, but reneged.) The government spent much of this money (in the form of notes) in New England. When these banks presented the Midwestern notes for redemption, the government, further shirking from its self-procaimed duties, declared "banking holidays," and allowed the wildcat banks to renege on their obligations for several years. The consequent exuberant policies which these banks followed gave private banking a bad name, and provided the government with a justification for taking over. These private banks were encouraged in their counterfeiting operations by the government itself.

At this stage of development, there was only one fly in the ointment, and it led the government to take the seventh step. Some countries engaged in counterfeiting, and hence inflation, to a greater degree than others. But when one country engages in a greater degree of counterfeiting-inflation than other countries, it becomes enmeshed in balance of payment problems. If country A's government counterfeits at a greater rate than country B's government, prices will rise faster in A than in B. A will find it easy to buy from B and hard to sell to B. Thus A's imports (what it buys) will outstrip its exports (what it sells). The immediate result of the imbalance between imports and exports will be a flow of gold from A to B to pay for the excess in purchases. But, because gold is limited, this cannot go on forever.

There are several possible responses. Government A could set a tax on imports (a tariff), or B could set a tax on exports. Quotas could be set by both countries prohibiting trade beyond a certain point. A could *devalue* its currency, making it easier for it to export, and harder for it to import. Or, B could *revalue* its currency, with the opposite effects. There are problems, however, with all of these responses. Tariffs and quotas interfere with trade, specialization, and the international division of labor. Devaluations and revaluations are very disruptive and interfere with the system of international trade which the world has spent so many years building. In addition, they do not really solve the problem of imbalance, and currency crises are bound to recur every time changes in the relative value of the various currencies of the world occur.

The world is now undergoing this seventh step, hence, it is difficult to trace it to its conclusion. Two patterns, however, seem to be emerging. One is the advent of a world monetary conference of which Bretton Woods is an example. At conferences of this type, the leading counterfeiter-inflationists gather to discuss possible remedies for their actions (although of course they do not see their role in this way). They usually discuss adopting some version of the central banking system of the United States for worldwide use. Suggestions have been made for an international equivalent of our Federal Reserve System. A strong world bank of this type would have much the same power over the entire world that a national bank has over its own country. It would have the power to force all banks to inflate in unison, and to direct the inflation to ensure that no power but itself shall be able to counterfeit money. Because each nationalistic counterfeiting center has so far jealously guarded its own powers, such a world central bank has not yet come into existence.

An alternative system, popularized by Milton Friedman of the University of Chicago, is the system of "flexible exchange rates." This system operates in such a way that whenever the prices or value of two countries' currencies fall out of line with one another, they automatically readjust. That is, the currency prices of the various countries are allowed to change in terms of one another. This is in significant contrast to the agreements made at previous world monetary conferences, in which these prices are *fixed* in terms of each other. With a flexible system, if country A inflates at a higher rate than country B, there will be a relative excess supply of the currency of A, which will drive its price down, choke off its imports, and make its exports more attractive. The great advantage of the flexible exchange system over the fixed exchange systems of the world monetary agreements is that it is an entirely *automatic* system. Thus the crises which would occur under a fixed system every time currencies change value with respect to one another are avoided.

However, since both these systems are only superficial attempts to suppress the ill effects which result from government counterfeit-inflationary schemes, neither can be favored.

Paradoxically, these ill effects are *good* things. Just as a pain in the body can be a warning of a far more serious condition, and is, therefore, beneficial, a balance of payments problem can be a signal of the menace of international inflation. Attempting to paper over these difficulties with flexible exchange rate schemes leaves the world's economy open to the ravages of inflation. It would be far better for the economy of the world, and for every individual country, if instead of devising ways to prop up counterfeiting and the resultant inflation, the governments of the world gave up these policies altogether.

In this connection, one cannot help daydreaming about Treasury agents, the "T" men of modern television serials. Dedicated to the elimination of counterfeiting, dressed in the best "FBI modern" style, they represent the essence of "uncorruptible" (ho, ho), tough law enforcers. On television their adventures usually begin with an overview of them walking down the steps of the Treasury Building. Were they to turn around, and walk back *up* the steps, and back *into* the offices of their superiors, and arrest *them*, they would be corralling perhaps the biggest gang of counterfeiters the world has ever known.

As to the claim that the private counterfeiter is a hero, three criteria for heroic actions must be applied. The act must not violate the rights of innocent people; the act must be of great benefit to large numbers of people; and it must be performed at great personal risk.

There can be no doubt regarding the third point. Nongovernmental counterfeiters operate at great risk to themselves. The government has declared such activity illegal. The Treasury Department spends large sums of money to apprehend private counterfeiters. The government stands ready to prosecute all those accused of counterfeiting, and to jail all who are found guilty. It cannot be doubted that the "risk" criterion is more than amply met.

Furthermore, it is clear that the activities of private counterfeiters are beneficial to the public. Nongovernmental counterfeiting, if allowed to be pursued, would spell the ruin of the government's own system of counterfeit money. The extent to which nongovernment counterfeiters are active is the extent to which the effectiveness of the government's own counterfeit system is decreased. The fact that the government's counterfeit system is very harmful constitutes in itself a strong *prima facie* case for nongovernment counterfeiting. (Of course, private counterfeiting is illegal, and cannot, therefore, be advocated. Still it is of interest to spin out the implications of economic theory.)

It may be objected that if private counterfeiters gained power, and replaced the government, the people would be no better off. This, of course, is true. But the fact is that private counterfeiters are "small time," and will undoubtedly remain so. They could pose no more than a minor problem. It is in fact this reality which clinches the argument for private counterfeiters. They do not pose a threat to the people; they are not, nor are they likely to become strong enough to do that. The effect they have is to reduce and counteract the great evil of government counterfeiting. This is beneficial for great numbers of people. Although a few individuals may suffer a loss from this activity, on balance, the activity of the private counterfeiter is more beneficial than harmful. And, it must be remembered, their activity is not fraudulent and hence immoral, since they do *not* seek to pass off counterfeit money for genuine.

15

THE MISER

The miser has never recovered from Charles Dickens' attack on him in *A Christmas Carol*. Although the miser had been sternly criticized before Dickens, the depiction of Ebenezer Scrooge has become definitive and has passed into the folklore of our time. Indeed, the attitude pervades even in freshman economics textbooks. There the miser is roundly condemned and blamed for unemployment, changes in the business cycle, and economic depressions and recessions. In the famous—or rather infamous—"paradox of savings," young students of economics are taught that, although saving may be sensible for an individual or a family, it may be folly for the economy as a whole. The prevalent Keynesian doctrine holds that the more saving in an economy, the less spending for consumption, and the less spending, the fewer jobs.

It is time that an end be put to all these misconceptions. Many and various benefits are derived from saving. Ever since the first caveman saved seed corn for future planting, the human race has owed a debt of gratitude to the hoarders, misers, and savers. It is to those people who refused to use up at once their entire store of wealth and chose rather to *save* it for a needy time, that we owe the capital equipment which enables us to aspire to a civilized standard of living. It is true, of course, that such people became richer than their fellows, and perhaps thereby earned their enmity. Perhaps the whole process of saving and accumulating was cast into disrepute along with the saver. But the enmity is not deserved. For the wages earned by the masses are intimately dependent upon the rate at which the saver can accumulate money. There are, for example, many reasons contributing to the fact that the American worker earns more than, say, his Bolivian counterpart. The American worker's education, health, and motivation play important roles. But a *major* contribution to the wage differential is the greater amount of capital stored up by American employers than by Bolivians. And this is not an exceptional case. The saver has been instrumental throughout history in lifting the pack above the level of the savage.

Perhaps it will be objected that there is a difference between *saving* (acknowledged to be productive in the process of capital accumulation), and *hoarding* (withholding money from consumption spending), and that the saver channels his money into capital goods industries where they can do some good; hoarded money is completely barren. The hoarder, it will be claimed, reduces the money received by retailers, forcing them to fire employees and reduce orders from jobbers. Jobbers in turn are forced to reduce their staff and to cut back on orders from wholesalers. The whole process, under the influence of hoarders, will be repeated throughout the entire structure of production. As employees are fired, they will have less to spend on consumption goods, thus compounding the process. Hoarding is thus seen as completely sterile and destructive.

The argument is plausible except for a crucial point which this Keynesian-inspired argument fails to take into account— the possibility of changes in prices. Before a retailer begins to lay off employees and cut back on orders because of unsold goods, he will usually try lowering his prices. He will hold a sale or use some other technique which will be equivalent to a decrease in price. Unless his troubles are due to the unsalability of his wares,

"Lip up, will ya', Edith! You knew I wasn't a Keynesian when you married me!"

this will suffice to end the vicious circle of unemployment and depression. How so?

In withholding money from the consumer's market, and *not* making it available for the purchase of capital equipment, the hoarder causes a decrease in the amount of money in circulation. The amount of available goods and services remains the same.

Since one of the most important determinants of price in any economy is the relationship between the amount of money and the amount of goods and services, the hoarder succeeds in lowering the level of prices. Consider a simplistic but not wholly inaccurate model in which all the dollars in the economy are bid against all its goods and services. Thus the fewer the dollars, the greater the purchasing power of each. Since hoarding can be defined as reducing the amount of money in circulation, and, other things equal, less money means lower prices, it can readily be seen that hoarding leads to lower prices.

There is no harm in lowering the level of prices. Quite the contrary, one of the great benefits is that all other people, the nonmisers, benefit from cheaper goods and services.

Nor will lower prices cause depressions. Indeed, the course of the prices of some of our most successful machinery has followed a strong downward curve. When cars, televisions, and computers were first produced, they were priced far beyond the reach of the average consumer. But technical efficiency succeeded in lowering prices until they were within the reach of the mass of consumers. Needless to say, neither a depression nor recession was caused by these falling prices. In fact, the only businessmen who suffer in the face of such a trend are those who follow the Keynesian analysis and do not lower their prices in the face of falling demand. But far from causing an ever widening depression, as the Keynsenians contend, such businessmen only succeed in driving themselves into bankruptcy. For the rest, business continues as satisfactorily as before, but with a lower price level. The cause of depressions, therefore, exists elsewhere.[1]

There is likewise no substance in the objection to hoarding on the ground that it is disruptive, and continually forces the economy to adjust. Even if true, it would not constitute an indictment of hoarding, for the free market is preeminently an

---

[1]See Murray N. Rothbard, *America's Great Depression* (New Rochelle, N.Y.: Van Nostrand, 1963).

institution of adjustment and reconciliation of divergent and ever-changing tastes. To criticize hoarding on this ground, one would also have to criticize changing clothing styles as well, for they continually call on the market for "fine tuning" adjustment. Hoarding is not even a very disruptive process because for every miser stuffing money into his mattress, there are numerous misers' heirs ferreting it out. This has always been the case, and it is not likely to change drastically.

Claims that the miser's hoard of cash is sterile because it does not draw interest as it would if it were banked is also without merit. Could the money held by individuals in their wallets be characterized as sterile since it does not draw interest either? If people voluntarily forbear to earn interest on their money and instead hold it in cash balances, the money may appear useless from our point of view, but it undoubtedly is not useless from theirs. The miser may want his money not for later spending, not to bridge the gap between expenditures and payments, but rather for the pure *joy* of holding cash balances. How can the economist, educated in the utility maximization tradition, characterize *joy as sterile?* Art lovers who hoard rare paintings and sculpture are not characterized as engaging in a sterile enterprise. People who own dogs and cats, solely for the purpose of enjoyment and not investment, are not described as engaging in sterile activity. Tastes differ among people, and what is sterile for one person may be far from sterile for another.

The miser's hoarding of large cash balances can only be considered heroic. We benefit from lowered price levels, which result from it. The money which we have and are willing to spend becomes more valuable, enabling the purchaser to buy more with the same amount of money. Far from being harmful to society, the miser is a benefactor, increasing our buying power each time he engages in hoarding.

16

THE INHERITOR

Heirs and heiresses are usually depicted as irresponsible, idle, lazy individuals who enjoy lives of unearned luxury. This is perhaps a true characterization of many in the class. But it does not detract from the heroic role played by the inheritor.

An inheritance is simply a form of gift—a gift that is given upon death. Like gifts that are given upon births, birthdays, weddings, anniversaries, and holidays, it can be defined as the voluntary transfer of considerations from one party to another. One cannot, therefore, oppose inheritances, and at the same time favor other types of gifts. Yet, many people do just that. Their anti-inheritance bias is spurred on by images of thieves who pass on their ill-gotten gains to their children. They see members of the ruling class accumulating fortunes, not through honest trade, but through government subsidies, tariffs, and licensing protections, and passing on what they have accumulated. Surely this should be prohibited. The elimination of an inheritance seems to be a solution.

It would, however, be impossible to eliminate inheritance unless all other types of gifts were also eliminated. The 100 percent tax on inheritance, often suggested as the means by which

117

"Get lost, Creep!"

to eliminate inheritance, would not accomplish this. For if other types of gifts were permitted, the tax could easily be circumvented. Money and property could simply be transferred by means of birthday gifts, Christmas gifts, etc. Parents might even have gifts held in trust for their children, to be turned over on the child's first birthday after the death of the parent.

The solution to the problem of illicitly earned wealth, white-collar and otherwise, does not lie in preventing the next generation from obtaining the ill-gotten funds, but in making certain that these funds are not retained in the first place. Attention should rather be focused on retrieving the illicit property and returning it to the victim.

Will it be argued that the 100 percent inheritance tax is a "second best" policy? That since we do not have power to strip the criminals of their ill-gotten gains, efforts should be made to deny them the opportunity of passing the fortunes on to their children? This is contradictory. If the power is lacking to bring criminals to justice because white-collar criminals control the system of justice, then clearly there is a lack of power to impose a 100 percent inheritance tax on them.

In fact, even if such a tax could be enacted and enforced, the yearning for egalitarianism which really animates all such proposals would be frustrated. For true egalitarianism means not only an equal distribution of money, but also an equal distribution of nonmonetary considerations. How would the egalitarians remedy the inequities between those who are sighted and those who are blind, those who are musically talented and those who are not, those who are beautiful and those who are ugly, those who are gifted and those who are not? What of the inequities between those who have happy dispositions and those who are prone to melancholy? How would the egalitarians mediate them? Could money be taken from those who have "too much happiness" and given to those who have "too little" as compensation? How much is a happy disposition worth? Would $10.00 per year trade at par for five units of happiness?

The ludicrousness of such a position might lead the egalitarians to adopt a "second best" policy, such as the one used by the dictator in "Harrison Bergeron," a short story in *Welcome to the Monkey House* by Kurt Vonnegut.[1] In the story, strong people were forced to carry weights in order to bring them down to the

---

[1]Kurt Vonnegut, *Welcome to the Monkey House* (New York: Dell, 1970).

level of the rest of the people; musically inclined individuals were forced to wear earphones that gave forth shockingly loud sounds in proportion to their musical talent. This is where the desire for egalitarianism logically leads. The elimination of monetary inheritance is but the first step.

It is the inheritor and the institution of inheritance that stands between civilization as we know it and a world in which no talent or happiness is allowed to mar equality. If individuality and civilization are valued, the inheritor will be placed on the pedestal he richly deserves.

17

THE MONEYLENDER

Ever since Biblical times, when the moneylenders were driven from the temple, they have been scorned, criticized, vilified, persecuted, prosecuted, and caricatured. Shakespeare, in *The Merchant of Venice*, characterized the moneylender as a Jew scurrying around trying to exact his "pound of flesh." In the movie, *The Pawnbroker*, the moneylender was an object of loathing.

The moneylender, however, together with his first cousins, the usurer, the pawnbroker, and the loan shark, have been badly misjudged. Although they perform a necessary and important service, they are, nevertheless, extremely unpopular.

Lending and borrowing take place because people differ as to their *rate of time preference* (the rate at which they are willing to trade money they presently possess, for money they will receive in the future). Mr. A may be anxious to have money *right now*, and not care too much about what money he may have in the future. He is willing to give up $200 *next year* in order to have $100 *now*. Mr. A has a very *high* rate of time preference. At the other end of the spectrum are the people with very *low* rates of time preference. To them, "future money" is almost as important as "present money." Mr. B, with a low rate of time preference, is willing to give up only $102 next year in order to receive

$100 now. Unlike Mr. A, who cares much more about present money than future money, Mr. B would not give up a large amount of future money for cash in hand. (It should be noted that a negative time preference does not exist, that is, a preference for money in the future over money in the present. This would be equivalent to saying that there would be a preference toward giving up $100 in the present, in order to get $95 in the future. This is irrational unless there are conditions other than time preference which operate. For example, one might want to purchase protection for money that is unsafe now, but will be safe a year hence, etc. Or, one may want to savor his dessert and postpone consumption until after dinner. "Dessert-before-dinner" would then be considered a *different* good than "dessert-after-dinner," no matter how similar the two goods were in physical terms. There is thus no preference shown for a good in the future over the *same* good in the present.)

Although it is not necessary, it is usual for a person with a high time preference (Mr. A), to become a net *borrower* of money, and for a person with a low time preference (Mr. B), to become a *lender*. It would be natural, for example, for Mr. A to borrow from Mr. B. Mr. A is willing to give up $200 a year from now in order to get $100 now, and Mr. B would be willing to loan $100 now if he can get at least $102 after one year has elapsed. If they agree that $150 is to be repaid a year hence for a present loan of $100, they both gain. Mr. A will gain the difference between the $200 he would have been willing to pay for $100 now and the $150 that he will actually be called upon to pay. That is, he will gain $50. Mr. B will gain the difference between the $150 that he will actually get a year hence and the $102 that he would have been willing to accept in a year for giving up the $100 now, a gain of $48. In fact, because moneylending is a trade, like any other trade, both parties must gain or they would refuse to participate.

A moneylender may be defined as someone who loans out his own money or the money of others. In the latter case his function is that of intermediary between the lender and borrower. In either case, the moneylender is as honest as any other businessman. He does not force anyone to do business with him nor is he himself compelled. There are, of course, dishonest moneylenders just as there are dishonest people in all walks of life. But there is nothing dishonest or reprehensible about moneylending *per se*. Some criticism of this view deserves further examination.

1. "Moneylending is infamous because it is frequently accompanied by violence. Borrowers (or victims) unable to pay their debts are often found murdered—usually by the loan shark." Individuals who borrow money from moneylenders usually have contracts with them to which they have fully agreed. One is hardly a victim of a moneylender if one has agreed to repay a loan, and then reneges on the contractual promise. On the contrary, the moneylender is the victim of the borrower. If the loan, but not the repayment is consummated, the situation is equivalent to theft. There is little difference between the thief who breaks into the moneylender's office and steals money, and the person who "borrows" it contractually, and then refuses to pay it back. In both cases, the result is the same—someone has taken possession of money which is not theirs.

Killing a debtor is an unjust overreaction, just as the murder of a thief would be. The primary reason moneylenders take the law into their own hands, however, and do not hesitate to use forceful means, even murder, is that moneylending is controlled by the underworld. But this control came about virtually at the public's request! When courts refuse to compel debtors to pay their rightful debts, and they prohibit the lending of money at high rates of interest, the underworld steps in. Whenever the government outlaws a commodity for which there are consumers, be it whiskey, drugs, gambling, prostitution, or high interest loans, the underworld enters the industry that law-abiding entrepreneurs fear to service. There is nothing in whiskey, drugs, gambling, prostitution, or moneylending that is intrinsically criminal. It is solely because of a legal prohibition that gangland methods become associated with these fields.

2. "Money is sterile and produces nothing by itself. Therefore, any interest charge for its use is exploitative. Moneylenders,

who charge abnormal interest rates, are among the most exploitative people in the economy. They richly deserve the opprobrium they receive."

Apart from the ability of money to buy goods and services, having money earlier, rather than later, provides an escape from the pain of waiting for fulfillment. It fosters a productive investment which, at the end of the loan period, even after paying the interest charge, yields more goods and services than at the beginning.

As for the "exorbitantly high" rates of interest, it should be understood that in a free market, the rate of interest tends to be determined by the time preferences of all the economic actors. If the rate of interest is inordinately high, forces will tend to develop which will push it down. If, for example, the rate of interest is higher than the time preference rate of the people involved, the demand for loans will be less than the supply, and the interest rate will be forced down. If the interest rate shows no tendency to decrease, this indicates not that it is too high, but that only a high rate of interest can equilibrate the demand for loans, and satisfy the time preference rate of the economic actors.

The critic of high interest rates has in mind a "fair" rate of interest. But a "fair" rate of interest or a "just" price does not exist. This is an atavistic concept, a throwback to medieval times when monks debated the question, along with the question of how many angels can fit on the head of a pin. If there is any meaning to the "fair" rate of interest doctrine, it can only be the rate which is mutually agreeable to two consenting adults, and that is exactly what the market rate of interest is.

3. "Moneylenders prey upon the poor by charging higher rates of interest than they charge other borrowers."

It is a common myth that the rich compose virtually the whole moneylending class and that the poor virtually all the borrowing class. This, however, is not true. What determines whether a person becomes a net borrower or lender is his rate of time preference, not his income. Rich corporations that sell bonds are borrowers, for the sale of bonds represents money

"I'm not surprised. Only yesterday the 'Journal' reported that the default rate on loans was up 8.9% over the first quarter."

borrowed. Most wealthy people who own real estate or other properties which are heavily mortgaged, are almost certainly net borrowers, not net lenders. On the other hand, every poor widow or pensioner with a small bank account is a moneylender.

It is true that moneylenders charge the poor higher rates of interest than they charge other people, but when stated in this way it can be misleading. For moneylenders charge higher rates of interest to individuals who are greater risks—those who are less likely to repay the loan—regardless of wealth.

One way to decrease the risk of default and, therefore, the rate of interest charged, is to put up collateral or real property that would be forfeited if the loan is not repaid. Since rich people are more capable of putting up collateral for loans than poor people, their loans are granted at lower rates of interest. The reason, however, is not because they are rich, but because the lender is less likely to undergo losses in case of default.

There is nothing untoward or unique about this situation. Poor people pay a higher rate for fire insurance since their houses have less fireproofing than rich people's houses. They are charged more for medical care since they are less healthy. Food costs are higher for poor people because there is more crime in their neighborhoods, and crime raises the cost of conducting a business. This is, to be sure, regrettable, but it is not the result of malice against the poor. The moneylender, like the health insurance company and the grocer, seeks to protect his investment.

Imagine the results of a law which prohibits *usury*, which can be defined as charging a rate of interest higher than the lawmaker approves of. Since the poor and not the rich pay the higher interest rate, the law would have its first effects on them. The effect would be to *hurt the poor*, and, if anything, *enhance the rich*. The law seems to be designed to protect the poor from having to pay high interest rates, but in reality it would really make it impossible for them to borrow money at all! If the moneylender must choose between loaning money to the poor at rates he regards as too low, and not loaning them any money at all, it is not difficult to see what choice he will make.

What will the moneylender do with the money he would have loaned to the poor but for the prohibitory law? He will make loans exclusively to the rich, incurring little risk of nonrepayment. This will have the effect of lowering the interest rates for the rich, because the greater the supply of a good in any given market, the lower the price. The question of whether or not it is fair to prohibit exorbitant rates of interest is not now under discussion, only the effects of such a law. And these effects are, quite clearly, calamitous for the poor.

18

THE NONCONTRIBUTOR TO CHARITY

We are beset by the view that it is blessed to give to charity. That it is also virtuous, seemly, good, fair, respectable, altruistic, and endearing. In like manner, the refusal to give to charity is met with contempt, derision, incredulity, and horror. The person who refuses to contribute to charity is considered a pariah.

This sociological imperative is supported by legions of beggars, fundraisers, clerics, and other "needy" groups. We are exhorted from the pulpit and the media, by the Hare Krishnas and the panhandlers, the flower people and the March of Dimes children, the cripples, the helpless, the impoverished, and the beaten down.

Contributing to charity is not in itself evil. When it is a voluntary decision on the part of responsible adults, it does not violate an individual's rights. Yet there are dangers in charity, and compelling reasons for refusing to contribute to it. In addition, there are serious flaws in the moral philosophy upon which charity is based.

THE EVILS OF CHARITY

One of the great evils of charity, and one of the most cogent reasons for refusing to contribute to it, is that it interferes with the

129

survival of the human species. According to the Darwinian principle of the "survival of the fittest," those organisms most able to exist in a given environment will be "naturally selected" (by showing a greater propensity to live until the age of procreation, and thus be more likely to leave offspring). One result, in the long run, is a species whose members have a greater ability to survive. This does not imply that the strong "kill off" the weak, as has been alleged. It merely suggests that the strong will be more successful than the weak in the procreation of the species. Thus the ablest perpetuate themselves and the species thrives.

Some contend that the law of natural selection does not apply to modern civilization. Critics point to artificial kidney machines, open heart surgery, and other scientific and medical breakthroughs, and argue that Darwin's survival law has been preempted by modern science. For people with diseases and genetic drawbacks, which in the past led to an early death, today live on to reproduce.

This does not, however, demonstrate that the Darwinian law is inapplicable. Modern scientific breakthroughs have not "repealed" Darwin's law, they have only changed the specific cases to which it applies.

In the past, the characteristic antithetical to human survival might have been a defective heart or poor kidneys. But with the advent of modern medical advances, medical failures are likely to become less and less important as grounds for natural selection. What will become more and more important is the ability to live on a crowded planet. Characteristics opposed to survival may include an allergy to smoke, excessive argumentativeness, or bellicosity. Such characteristics will tend to lessen a person's ability to survive to adulthood. These characteristics lessen the person's chances of maintaining a situation (marriage, employment) in which reproduction is possible. Thus, if the Darwinian laws are allowed to work themselves out, such negative traits will tend to disappear. But if charity is extended, these harmful traits will be carried over to the next generation.

"Go inherit your own money!"

While charity of this type is undeniably harmful, when it is private, it is limited in scope by a type of Darwinian law that applies to the givers: they come to bear some of the harm they cause. Thus they are led, as if by Adam Smith's "invisible hand" to cut back on their giving. For example, if parental charity takes the form of "sparing the rod and spoiling the child," some of the harmful effects of this charity rebound upon the parents. Being on the receiving end of spoiled children tends to temper the giver. (Many of the parents who supported their adult "hippie" children throughout the sixties discontinued such support when they themselves suffered from its harmful effects.) Private charity also has a built-in limitation because any given private fortune is circumscribed. The case of public charity is ominously different.

In public charity, all natural barriers are virtually absent. It is a rare case indeed when public charity is reduced because of its harmful effects. The fortune at the goverment's disposal is only limited by its desire for taxes and its ability to levy them on an unwilling public.

A case in point is the American foreign aid program of the 1950s and 1960s. The government of the United States paid American farmers more than the market price for their produce, thus creating gigantic surpluses, for which still more money had to be allotted. Large quantities of this produce were then sent to countries such as India, where the domestic farm industry was virtually ruined by this subsidized importation.

Other detrimental effects of governmental "charity" have been documented by a number of social scientists. G. William Domhoff in his book *The Higher Circles*,[1] shows that "charitable" institutions such as workmen's compensation, collective bargaining in labor, unemployment insurance, and welfare programs were begun not by advocates of the poor, as is universally accepted, but by the rich. These programs promote their own class interests. The aim of this state-corporate charity system is not to redistribute wealth from rich to poor, but to buy up the potential leaders of the poor and tie them to the hegemony of the ruling class, while maintaining an intellectual class determined to convince an unwary public that government charity actually benefits them.

In like manner, Piven and Cloward point out in *Regulating the Poor*[2] that the "charitable" institution of welfare serves not mainly to aid the poor, but rather to suppress them. The *modus operandi* here is to allow the welfare rolls to increase not in times

---

[1]G. William Domhoff, *The Higher Circles* (New York: Random House, 1970.)

[2]Frances F. Piven and Richard A. Cloward, *Regulating the Poor* (New York: Random House, 1971).

of great need, but in times of social upheaval, and to decrease the welfare rolls not in times of plenty, but in times of social tranquility. Thus the welfare system is a kind of "bread and circus" method of controlling the masses.

THE PHILOSOPHY BEHIND CHARITY

Despite these problems, there are those who view charity as a blessed state, and consider contributions a moral obligation. Such people would make charity compulsory, if they could. If, however, an act is made compulsory, it is not charity, for charity is defined as *voluntary* giving. If an individual is *forced* to give, he is not a contributor to charity, he is the victim of a robbery.

The crux of charity, for those who would wish it to be made compulsory, the laws of logic and linguistics notwithstanding, is that there is a duty, an obligation, a moral imperative, for all to give to the less fortunate. This rests on the premise that "we are each our brother's keepers."

This philosophy, however, contradicts a basic premise of morality—namely, that it should always be at least *possible* for a person to do what is moral. If there are two people in different geographical areas who are in dire need of John's aid *at the same time*, it would be impossible for John to help *both* of them. If John *cannot* help both needy people, and since helping both is a requirement of the brother's keeper morality, then clearly, with the best intentions, John *cannot* be moral. And if, according to any given theory of ethics, a well-intentioned person cannot be moral, the theory is incorrect.

The second basic flaw in the brother's keeper moral view is that it logically calls for *absolute income equality*, whether or not its proponents realize this. Remember, this morality preaches that it is the moral duty of those who have more, to share with those who have less. Adam, who has $100, shares with Richard, who has only $5, by giving Richard $10. Adam now has $90 and Richard $15. One might think that Adam has followed the dictates of the sharing philosophy. However, this philosophy states that it is the duty of all people to share with the less fortunate, and Adam *still* has more than Richard. If Adam wishes to act morally, according to the brother's keeper moral view, he will have to share again with Richard. The sharing can end only when Richard no longer has less than Adam.

The doctrine of absolute income equality, a necessary consequence of the brother's keeper philosophy, will admit of no prosperity for anyone over and above the meager pittance the most helpless individual is able to amass. Thus the brother's keeper philosophy is in direct and irreconcilable opposition to the natural ambition to improve one's lot. Believers in it are torn by ultimately conflicting views and the result, naturally enough, is hypocrisy. How else can one describe people who claim to be *practitioners* of the brother's keeper philosophy, and yet have well-stocked pantries, a television, a stereo set, a car, jewelry, and real estate, while in many parts of the world people face starvation? They dogmatically affirm their commitment to equality, yet deny that their lush wealth is in any way contradictory to this commitment.

One explanation offered is that a certain amount of wealth and well-being is necessary for them to maintain their jobs, which allows them to earn the money to contribute to the less fortunate. Clearly, it is true that the brother's keeper must maintain his own ability to "keep" his brothers. His demise due to starvation is not called for by the brother's keeper philosophy.

The wealthy brother's keeper thus explains himself as being in a position similar to the slave owned by the "rational" slave owner. For the slave must be at least minimally healthy and comfortable, even contented, if he or she is to produce for the owner. The wealthy brother's keeper has, in effect, enslaved *himself* for the benefit of the downtrodden whom he aids. He has amassed the amount which he needs in order to best serve his fellow man. His wealth and standard of living are just what a rational profit-maximizing slave owner would allow his slave to enjoy. Everything in his possession is enjoyed only to the extent, and for the sole purpose of, increasing and/or maintaining his economic ability to help those who are less fortunate than he is, according to this argument.

It might be barely possible that a brother's keeper living in a garret *could* be telling the truth when he explains his possessions in these terms. But what of the average person who claims to practice the brother's keeper morality—the civil servant earning $17,000 a year, and living in a cooperative apartment in New York City? It can hardly be seriously contended that the possessions he has collected are necessary for his productivity—especially when these holdings could be sold for money which could significantly aid the downtrodden.

Far from being a blessed activity, contributing to charity can have harmful effects. In addition, the moral theory upon which charity rests is riddled with contradictions and makes hypocrites of those who are pressured by it.

VI. BUSINESS AND TRADE

19

THE CURMUDGEON

Imagine, if you will, the problems of the real estate developer who is trying to supplant a city block of crumbling tenements with a modern residential complex, replete with gardens, swimming pools, balconies, and other accoutrements of comfortable living. Many problems arise, some by governmental obstacles (zoning laws, licensing requirements, bribes for acceptance of architectural plans). Nowadays, these are widespread, and stultifying. However, in some cases, an even greater problem is posed by the curmudgeon who owns and lives in the most decrepit tenement on the block. He is overly fond of his building and refuses to sell at any price. The builder offers preposterous sums of money, but the curmudgeon steadfastly refuses.

The curmudgeon, who may be a little old lady or a bitter old man, has long been active defending his homestead against the inroads of highway builders, railroad magnates, mining companies, or dam and irrigation control projects. Indeed, the plots of many western movies are based on this resistance. The curmudgeon and his spiritual soulmates served as the inspiration for the enactment of eminent domain legislation. He has been portrayed as a staunch human barrier to progress, with feet planted firmly at the crossroads, and his motto a strident, defiant "no."

Cases like this abound, and are said to demonstrate the curmudgeon's interference with the progress and well-being of the multitude. This popular view, however, is mistaken. The curmudgeon, who is depicted as standing in the way of progress, actually represents one of the greatest hopes that progress ever had—the institution of property rights. For the abuse heaped upon him is a disguised attack on the concept of private property itself.

Now if private property means anything, it means that owners have the right to make decisions with regard to the use of their property, as long as this use does not interfere with other property owners and their rights to the use of their own property. In the case of eminent domain, when the state forces the property owner to give up the rights to his property on terms that he would not voluntarily choose, the rights to private property are abridged.

The two primary arguments for private property are the moral and the practical. According to the moral argument, each man is, first of all, the complete owner of himself, and of the fruits of his labor. The principle behind his ownership of himself and his artifacts is the principle of homesteading or *natural* governance. Each person is the natural owner of himself because, in the nature of things, *his* will controls his actions. According to the principle of homesteading, each man owns his own person, and he therefore owns the things which he produces—those parts of nature hitherto unowned and which, when mixed with his labor, are transformed into productive entities. The only moral ways for these entities to change ownership are voluntary trade and voluntary gift-giving. These ways are consistent with the original owner's natural homesteading rights, for they are methods by which ownership is given up voluntarily, in accordance with the owner's will.

Let us assume that the property owned by the curmudgeon was gained by this process of natural homesteading. If so, there was an original homesteader, there were voluntary sales of the land or the land may have been given in the form of a gift at one time or another. The land then passed into the control of the curmudgeon through an unbroken chain of voluntary events, all consistent with the principle of homesteading; in other words, his land title would be legitimate.

Any attempt to wrest it from him without his consent thus violates the principle of homesteading, and hence is immoral. It is an act of aggression against an innocent party. (The question will be raised regarding land which has been stolen. In fact, *most* of the earth's surface meets this criteria. In such cases, if there is evidence that (1) the land has been stolen, and (2) another individual can be found who is the rightful owner or heir, this person's right of ownership must be respected. In all other cases, the actual owner must be considered the rightful owner. *De facto* ownership is sufficient when the owner is the original homesteader or when no other legitimate claimant can be found.)

Many recognize this when the curmudgeon resists the demands on his property by private business. It is clear that one private interest does not have the right to intrude upon another private interest. However, when it is the state, as represented by eminent domain laws, the case seems different. For the state, it is assumed, represents all the people, and the curmudgeon purportedly is blocking progress. Yet in many cases—if not all—governmental laws of eminent domain are used to further private interests. Many urban relocation programs, for example, are at the behest of private universities and hospitals. Much of the condemnation of private property by eminent domain laws is accomplished for the special interests of lobbies and other pressure groups. The condemnation of the land on which Lincoln Center for the Performing Arts in New York City was built is a case in point. This tract of land was condemned to make way for "high culture." People were forced to sell their land at prices the government was willing to pay. *Whose* culture this center serves is clear to anyone who reads the list of subscribers to Lincoln Center. It is a *Who's Who* of the ruling class.

In considering the second set of arguments for private property rights, the practical arguments, there is one based on the

"Enough, enough of this pleading and cajoling! As president
of the university I tell you this—we'll get your property for
our humanities building one way or another, so watch out!"

concept of *stewardship*. Under private stewardship, it is claimed,
property receives the "best" possible care. *Who* controls the piece
of property is not important. What is important is that all property be privately owned, that precise delineations between the

properties be clearly marked off, and that no forced or involuntary transfers of property be allowed. If these conditions are met, and a *laissez faire* market is maintained, those who "mishandle" their property lose profits they could otherwise earn, and those who nurture their property can accumulate funds. Thus, those better able to maintain a good stewardship eventually become responsible for more and more, since they can afford to buy up extra property with their earnings, while the poor stewards will have less and less. The general level of stewardship, therefore, will rise, and better care will be taken of property in general. The stewardship system, by rewarding good stewards and penalizing poor ones, increases the average level of stewardship. It does so automatically, without political votes, without political purges, and without fuss or fanfare.

What happens when the government steps in and props up, by means of loans and subsidies, failing enterprises managed by incompetents? The effectiveness of the stewardship system is vitiated, if not destroyed altogether. The failing enterprises are protected by government subsidies from the consequences of their mismanagement. Such government infringements take many forms—the granting of franchises, licenses, and other types of monopoly advantages to one select individual or group; the granting of tariffs and quotas to protect inefficient domestic "caretakers" against competition from more efficient foreign stewards; and the awarding of government contracts which pervert the original consumption wishes of the public. All perform the same function. They enable the government to interpose itself between a bad caretaker and a public which has chosen not to patronize him.

What if the government interposes itself in the opposite way? What if it tries to hasten the process by which good stewards acquire more and more property? Since the sign of good stewardship in a free market is success, why can't the government simply analyze the present distribution of property and wealth, ascertain who the successes and the failures are, and then complete the transfer of property from poor to wealthy? The answer is that the market system works *automatically*, making day-to-day adjustments in immediate response to the competence of the various stewards. Governmental attempts to hasten the process by transferring money and property from the poor to the rich can only be done on the basis of the *past* behavior of the stewards in question. But there is no guarantee that the future will resemble the past, that those who were successful entrepreneurs in the past will be successful entrepreneurs in the future! Similarly, there is no way of knowing who among the present poor have the innate competence to eventually succeed in a free market. Governmental programs, based as they would have to be on *past* accomplishments, would be arbitrary and inherently contrived.

Now the curmudgeon is a prototype of a "backward," poor individual, who is, by all standards, a bad manager. Thus he is a prime candidate for a governmental scheme whose goal is to speed up the market process by which good stewards acquire more property and bad stewards lose theirs. But this, as we have seen, is a scheme bound to fail.

The second practical defense of private property may be called the *praxeological* argument. This view focuses on the question of who is to evaluate transactions. According to it, the only scientific evaluation that can be made of a voluntary trade is that all parties to it gain in the *ex ante* sense. That is, at the time of the trade, both parties value what they will gain more than they value what they will give up in exchange. The parties would not voluntarily make the trade unless, at that time, each valued what is to be received more than what is to be given up. Thus a mistake in a trade will not be made in the *ex ante* sense. However, a mistake can be made in the *ex post* sense—after the trade has been completed, one can change one's evaluation. However, in most instances, the trade usually reflects the desires of both parties.

How is this relevant to the situation of the curmudgeon, who is charged with blocking progress and thwarting the natural transfer of property from the less able to the more able? According to the praxeologist, the answer to the question, "Shouldn't he be forced to sell his property to those who can manage it more productively?" is a resounding "no." The only evaluation that can be made, from a scientific perspective, is of a voluntary trade. A voluntary trade is, in the *ex ante* sense, good. If the curmudgeon refuses to trade, no negative evaluation is possible. All that can be said is that the curmudgeon values his property at more than the developer was willing or able to pay. Since no interpersonal comparisons of utility or welfare have scientific foundation (there is no unit by which such things can be measured, let alone compared between different people), there is no legitimate basis on which to say that the curmudgeon's refusal to sell his property is harmful or causes problems. True, the curmudgeon's choice serves to obstruct the real estate developer's goal. But then, the goals of the real estate developer are just as obstructive of the goals of the old curmudgeon. Clearly, the curmudgeon is under no obligation to frustrate his own desires in order to satisfy another's. Yet the curmudgeon is usually the object of unjustified censure and criticism as he continues to act with integrity and courage in the face of enormous social pressures. This must stop.

20

THE SLUMLORD

To many people, the slumlord—alias ghetto landlord and rent gouger—is proof that man can, while still alive, attain a satanic image. Recipient of vile curses, pincushion for needle bearing tenants with a penchant for voodoo, perceived as exploiter of the downtrodden, the slumlord is surely one of the most hated figures of the day. The indictment is manifold: he charges unconscionably high rents; he allows his buildings to fall into disrepair; his apartments are painted with cheap lead paint which poisons babies, and he allows junkies, rapists, and drunks to harass the tenants. The falling plaster, the overflowing garbage, the omnipresent roaches, the leaky plumbing, the roof cave-ins and the fires, are all integral parts of the slumlord's domain. And the only creatures who thrive in his premises are the rats.

The indictment, highly charged though it is, is spurious. The owner of ghetto housing differs little from any other purveyor of low cost merchandise. In fact, he is no different from any purveyor of any kind of merchandise. They all charge as much as they can.

First consider the purveyors of cheap, inferior, and second-hand merchandise as a class. One thing above all else stands out about merchandise they buy and sell: it is cheaply built, inferior in quality, or secondhand. A rational person would not expect high quality, exquisite workmanship, or superior new merchandise at bargain rate prices; he would not feel outraged and cheated if bargain rate merchandise proved to have only bargain rate qualities. Our expectations from margarine are not those of butter. We are satisfied with lesser qualities from a used car than from a new car. However, when it comes to housing, especially in the urban setting, people expect, even insist upon, quality housing at bargain prices.

But what of the claim that the slumlord overcharges for his decrepit housing? This is erroneous. *Everyone* tries to obtain the highest price possible for what he produces, and to pay the lowest price possible for what he buys. Landlords operate this way, as do workers, minority group members, socialists, babysitters, and communal farmers. Even widows and pensioners who save their money for an emergency try to get the highest interest rates possible for their savings. According to the reasoning which finds slumlords contemptible, all these people must also be condemned. For they "exploit" the people to whom they sell or rent their services and capital in the same way when they try to obtain the highest return possible. But, of course, they are not contemptible—at least not because of their desire to obtain as high a return as possible from their products and services. And neither are slumlords. Landlords of dilapidated houses are singled out for something which is almost a basic part of human nature—the desire to barter and trade and to get the best possible bargain.

The critics of the slumlord fail to distinguish between the desire to charge high prices, which everyone has, and the ability to do so, which not everyone has. Slumlords are distinct, not because they want to charge high prices, but because they can. The question which is, therefore, central to the issue—and which the critics totally disregard—is why this is so.

What usually stops people from charging inordinately high prices is the competition which arises as soon as the price and profit margin of any given product or service begins to rise. If the price of frisbees, for example, starts to rise, established manufacturers will expand production, new entrepreneurs will enter the industry, used frisbees will perhaps be sold in second-hand markets, etc. All these activities tend to counter the original rise in price. If the price of rental apartments suddenly began to rise because of a sudden housing shortage, similar forces would come into play. New housing would be built by established real estate owners and by new ones who would be drawn into the industry by the price rise. Old housing would tend to be renovated; basements and attics would be pressed into use. All these activities would tend to drive the price of housing down, and cure the housing shortage.

If landlords tried to raise the rents in the absence of a housing shortage, they would find it difficult to keep their apartments rented. For both old and new tenants would be tempted away by the relatively lower rents charged elsewhere. Even if landlords banded together to raise rents, they would not be able to maintain the rise in the absence of a housing shortage. Such an attempt would be countered by new entrepreneurs, not party to the cartel agreement, who would rush in to meet the demand for lower priced housing. They would buy existing housing, and build new housing. Tenants would, of course, flock to the non-cartel housing. Those who remained in the high price buildings would tend to use less space, either by doubling up or by seeking less space than before. As this occurs it would become more difficult for the cartel landlords to keep their buildings fully rented. Inevitably, the cartel would break up, as the landlords sought to find and keep tenants in the only way possible: by lowering rents. It is, therefore, specious to claim that landlords charge whatever they please. They charge whatever the market will bear, as does everyone else.

An additional reason for calling the claim unwarranted is that there is, at bottom, no really legitimate sense to the concept of overcharging. "Overcharging" can only mean "charging more than the buyer would like to pay." But since we would all really like to pay *nothing* for our dwelling space (or perhaps minus infinity, which would be equivalent to the landlord paying the *tenant* an infinite amount of money for living in his building), landlords

"Let's see, I have a nice 3 room apartment on the upper West Side—No, no Madam, not a speck of lead paint on the woodwork—it's been all chewed off."

who charge anything at all can be said to be overcharging. Everyone who sells at any price greater than zero can be said to be overcharging, because we would all like to pay nothing (or minus infinity) for what we buy.

Disregarding as spurious the claim that the slumlord over-charges, what of the vision of rats, garbage, falling plaster, etc.? Is the slumlord responsible for these conditions? Although it is fashionable in the extreme to say "yes," this will not do. For the problem of slum housing is not really a problem of slums or of housing at all. It is a problem of *poverty*—a problem for which the landlord cannot be held responsible. And when it is not the result of poverty, it is not a social problem at all.

Slum housing with all its horrors is not a problem when the inhabitants are people who can afford higher quality housing, but *prefer* to live in slum housing because of the money they can save thereby. Such a choice might not be a popular one, but other people's freely made choices which affect only them cannot be classified as a social problem. (If that could be done, we would all be in danger of having our most deliberate choices, our most cherished tastes and desires characterized as "social problems" by people whose taste differs from ours.)

Slum housing is a problem when the inhabitants live there of necessity—not wishing to remain there, but unable to afford anything better. Their situation is certainly distressing, but the fault does not lie with the landlord. On the contrary, he is providing a necessary service, given the poverty of the tenants. For proof, consider a law prohibiting the existence of slums, and, therefore, of slumlords, without making provisions for the slumdwellers in any other way, such as providing decent housing for the poor, or an adequate income to buy or rent good housing. The argument is that if the slumlord truly harms the slumdweller, then his elimination, *with everything else unchanged*, ought to increase the net well-being of the slum tenant. But the law would not accomplish this. It would greatly harm not only the slumlords but the slumdwellers as well. If anything, it would harm the slumdwellers even more, for the slumlords would lose only one of perhaps many sources of income; the slumdwellers would lose their very homes. They would be forced to rent more expensive dwelling space, with consequent decreases in the amount of money available for food, medicines, and other necessities. No. The problem is not the slumlord; it is poverty. Only if the slumlord were the *cause* of poverty could he be legitimately blamed for the evils of slum housing.

Why is it then, if he is no more guilty of underhandedness than other merchants, that the slumlord has been singled out for vilification? After all, those who sell used clothes to Bowery bums are not reviled, even though their wares are inferior, the prices high, and the purchasers poor and helpless. Instead of blaming the merchants, however, we seem to know where the blame lies—in the poverty and hopeless conditon of the Bowery bum. In like manner, people do not blame the owners of junk-yards for the poor condition of their wares or the dire straits of their customers. People do not blame the owners of "day-old bakeries" for the staleness of the bread. They realize, instead, that were it not for junkyards and these bakeries, poor people would be in an even worse condition than they are now in.

Although the answer can only be speculative, it would seem that there is a positive relationship between the amount of governmental interference in an economic arena, and the abuse and invective heaped upon the businessmen serving that arena. There have been few laws interfering with the "day-old bak-eries" or junkyards, but many in the housing area. The link between government involvement in the housing market and the plight of the slumlord's public image should, therefore, be pinpointed.

That there is strong and varied government involvement in the housing market cannot be denied. Scatter-site housing proj-ects, "public" housing and urban renewal projects, zoning ordi-nances and building codes, are just a few examples. Each of these has created more problems than it has solved. More hous-ing has been destroyed than created, racial tensions have been exacerbated, and neighborhoods and community life have been shattered. In each case, it seems that the spillover effects of bureaucratic red tape and bungling are visited upon the slum-lord. He bears the blame for much of the overcrowding engen-dered by the urban renewal program. He is blamed for not keep-ing his buildings up to the standards set forth in unrealistic building codes which, if met, would radically *worsen* the situation of the slumdweller. (Compelling "Cadillac housing" can only harm the inhabitants of "Volkswagen housing." It puts all housing out of the financial reach of the poor.)

Perhaps the most critical link between the government and the disrepute in which the slumlord is held is the rent control law. For rent control legislation changes the usual profit incentives, which put the entrepreneur in the *service* of his customers, to incentives which make him the direct enemy of his tenant-customers.

Ordinarily the landlord (or any other businessman) earns money by serving the needs of his tenants. If he fails to meet these needs, the tenants will tend to move out. Vacant apartments mean, of course, a loss of income. Advertising, rental agents, repairs, painting, and other conditions involved in rerenting an apartment mean extra expenditures. In addition, the landlord who fails to meet the needs of the tenants may have to charge lower rents than he otherwise could. As in other businesses, the customer is "always right," and the merchant ignores this dictum only at his own peril.

But with rent control the incentive system is turned around. Here the landlord can earn the greatest return *not* by serving his tenants well, but by mistreating them, by malingering, by refusing to make repairs, by insulting them. When the rents are legally controlled at rates below their market value, the landlord earns the greatest return not by serving his tenants, but by *getting rid of them*. For then he can replace them with higher paying non-rent-controlled tenants.

If the incentive system is turned around under rent control, it is the self-selection process through which entry to the landlord "industry" is determined. The types of people attracted to an occupation are influenced by the type of work that must be done in the industry. If the occupation calls (financially) for service to consumers, one type of landlord will be attracted. If the occupation calls (financially) for harassment of consumers, then quite a different type of landlord will be attracted. In other words, in many cases the reputation of the slumlord as cunning, avaricious, etc., might be well-deserved, but it is the rent control program *in the first place* which encourages people of this type to become landlords.

If the slumlord were prohibited from lording over slums, and if this prohibition were actively enforced, the welfare of the poor slumdweller would be immeasurably worsened, as we have seen. It is the prohibition of high rents, by rent control and similar legislation, that causes the deterioration of housing. It is the prohibition of low-quality housing, by housing codes and the like, that causes landlords to leave the field of housing. The result is that tenants have fewer choices, and the choices they have are of low quality. If landlords cannot make as much profit in supplying housing to the poor as they can in other endeavors, they will leave the field. Attempts to lower rents and maintain high quality through prohibitions only lower profits and drive slumlords out of the field, leaving poor tenants immeasurably worse off.

It should be remembered that the basic cause of slums is not the slumlord, and that the worst "excesses" of the slumlord are due to governmental programs, especially rent control. The slumlord does make a positive contribution to society; without him, the economy would be worse off. That he continues in his thankless task, amidst all the abuse and vilification, can only be evidence of his basically heroic nature.

21

THE GHETTO MERCHANT

"How dare he charge such outrageously high prices for such shoddy merchandise? The store is filthy, the service horrible, and the guarantees worthless. The installment buying will keep you in debt to them for the rest of your life. The customers of these leeches are among the poorest, the most financially naïve to be found anywhere. The only remedy is to prohibit the high prices, low quality products, the devious installment plans, and the general exploitation of poor people."

Such is the view of a majority of those who have spoken out on the ghetto merchant "problem." And indeed, it has a certain plausibility. After all, ghetto merchants are mainly rich and white and their customers are mainly poor minority group members. The merchandise sold in ghetto shops is often more expensive than that sold in other areas, and of inferior quality. However, the proposed solution, to compel ghetto merchants to follow the practices of nonghetto neighborhoods, will not work. Rather, such compulsion will hurt the people it is designed to help—the poor.

It is easy to argue that if you prohibit something that is bad, something good will follow. It is simple, but not always true. And it is clearly untrue in the case of the ghetto merchant and his business practices. This facile argument blithely ignores the causes of the problem—why prices are really higher in the ghetto.

Although at first glance it might *appear* that prices are higher in luxury neighborhoods than in the ghetto, this is due to the fact that stores in the ghettos and the luxury neighborhoods do not really sell the same goods. The quality of the merchandise sold is lower in the ghetto. This holds even in the case of seemingly identical merchandise. A bottle of Heinz ketchup, for example, might be priced higher in the luxury neighborhood, but the product being sold there is the ketchup, plus the decor of the store, delivery and other services, and the convenience of shopping close to home or at all hours of the day and night. These amenities are either lacking altogether in the ghetto shop, or are present in a lesser form. When they are taken into account, it is clear that the ghetto consumer gets less for his money than the consumer in a luxury neighborhood.

This must be true because the price charged by the ghetto merchant reflects "hidden" operating expenses which the nonghetto merchant does not have to contend with. In the ghetto, there are higher rates of theft and crime of all types. There is more damage by fire, and greater chance of damage from riots. All this increases the insurance premiums that the merchant must pay. And it increases the necessary expenditures on burglar alarms, locks and gates, guard dogs, private policemen, etc.

Given that the costs of doing business are higher in the ghetto, the prices charged there must be greater. If they were not, ghetto merchants would earn a smaller profit than those outside the ghetto and they would abandon the area for greener pastures. What keeps prices in the ghetto high is not the "greed" of the ghetto merchant; *all* merchants, inside the ghetto and out, are greedy. What keeps the prices in the ghetto high are the high costs of doing business in these areas.

In fact, there is a constant tendency for profits in different fields of endeavor to become equalized or to come to equilibrium (given the expected variation in profit risk, and other nonpecuniary advantages or disadvantages). And the situation of ghetto merchants exemplifies this tendency. When profits in area A are higher than those in area B, merchants are drawn from B to A. When, as a result, only a few merchants are left in area B, competition there decreases and profits rise. And, as more and more merchants arrive in area A, competition increases and profits fall. Thus, even if at some point, ghetto merchants realized greater profits than others, they could not continue to earn greater profits for long. If there were more profits to be made in the ghetto, merchants would be drawn there, and the resulting competition would tend to drive profits down to equilibrium. And, in response to the lessened competition outside the ghetto, profits there would rise to equilibrium.

THE GHETTO MERCHANT AS BENEFACTOR

The question of nonpecuniary advantages and disadvantages have not yet been dealt with. But they exist. And all the nonpecuniary advantages are on the side of the merchant located outside the ghetto. The ghetto merchant, apart from the risk he faces to life and property, must bear in addition, the scorn of an outraged public who are angry and resentful at *him* for, among other things, selling shoddy merchandise at high prices.

Because of the indignities suffered by the ghetto merchant, the equilibrium profit rate will be higher in the ghetto than outside. In other words, profits will remain stable at a point at which ghetto merchants earn a greater profit than other merchants, but not so much greater that it tempts other merchants to enter the ghetto. The merchants outside the ghetto will not be attracted to the ghetto by this extra profit because it will be less than sufficient to compensate them for the extra indignities and risks they would suffer as ghetto merchants. The merchants who remain in the ghetto are those who are least put off by the indignities and risks involved. For them, the extra profit is enough

compensation. In other words, there will be (and always is) a self-selection procedure whereby those with the greatest tolerance for the risks and indignities of the ghetto will be swayed by the extra profit to remain there. Those with the least tolerance will not be compensated by the extra profits and will head for greener (whiter) fields.

If the tolerance of the ghetto merchants decreases, the equilibrium profit rate will have to rise. If it does not rise, those among the ghetto merchants who have the least capacity to bear the indignities will leave. Competition will decrease, and the remaining merchants will be able to raise their prices and, hence, their profits. This rise in profits will be just enough to compensate the remaining merchants in the face of their heightened sensitivities. The reason, then, that prices are not higher than they are in the ghetto is that these merchants have a great ability to bear the risks, scorn, and abuse.

In the light of this, the ghetto merchant who charges outrageously high prices can be considered a benefactor. For it is his ability to withstand the pressures placed upon him that keeps prices in the ghetto no higher than they are. But for this ability, prices would be even higher.

Another startling aspect should be considered. The villain, if anyone, is not the ghetto merchant whose tolerance for outrages keeps prices *down*; the villain is, rather, those who heap scorn and abuse upon him and revile him for charging high prices for shoddy merchandise. It is these "nattering nabobs of negativism" who are instrumental in keeping ghetto prices up. It is these grumblers, usually local politicians and community "leaders," seeking power and a political base, who raise the equilibrium profit differential necessary to keep merchants in the ghetto. If they were to cease their ill-advised condemnations, the nonpecuniary disadvantages of merchandising in the ghetto would diminish along with the equilibrium price differential, and hence, ghetto prices. Paradoxical though it may be, those who are most vociferous in their complaints about the high prices charged by ghetto merchants are actually responsible for keeping those prices higher than they would otherwise be!

This analysis is not restricted to cases in which the ghetto community is Hispanic or black and the merchants are white. For the risks of theft, fire, and damage by vandalism and riots would cause a black or Puerto Rican merchant to charge higher prices too. And the resulting abuse to which he would be subject would drive the prices even higher. If anything, the minority member merchant would have a more painful criticism to bear—the charge that he is a traitor to his ethnic group. The analysis, then, will become even more applicable when and if blacks and Puerto Ricans begin to replace whites as ghetto merchants.

RESTRICTIONS CAN ONLY BE HARMFUL

The effect of a law prohibiting the ghetto merchant from charging higher prices than those charged elsewhere can now be appreciated. It would simply drive merchants out of the ghetto! Higher costs of doing business with no opportunity to recoup them through higher prices, means lower profits. No merchant would voluntarily remain in such a business situation. In fact, merchants will not remain in ghettos unless they can earn a higher profit than can be earned elsewhere, to compensate them for the nonpecuniary disadvantages.

If the prohibition was strictly enforced, virtually *all* the merchants would leave the ghetto and seek their fortunes elsewhere, with a minute fraction remaining. Customers would then be forced to queue up at whatever shops were available, thereby reducing costs and increasing revenues to the point at which the merchants might be compensated for the higher costs of operating in the ghetto. But this would mean that residents of the ghetto would have to wait in line for long periods of time in order to make a purchase. And it is more than likely that customers would heap even greater abuse upon ghetto merchants for the even poorer service they would be receiving. Such crowds might even prove uncontrollable. In such a situation, the few remaining merchants would be forced to shut down. The citizens of the ghetto, the community "leaders," pundits, and commentators, would then blame the ghetto merchants for leaving the community.

The departure of the ghetto merchants would cause pain and suffering on a truly monumental scale. Ghetto residents would be compelled to travel great distances to make purchases which were formerly made in their neighborhoods. They would pay slightly lower prices for goods of slightly higher quality, but these gains would be more than counteracted by the increased carfare, and time lost in transit. We know this because these options are *always* open to ghetto inhabitants. Since local people patronize neighborhood stores presently, they must feel they do better closer to home.

The ghetto dwellers could not even make deals with one another by which some would do the shopping for the rest. This would implicitly convert some of them to ghetto merchants, and the same choice would be open to these new ghetto merchants as were available to the old ones. There is no reason to suppose that they would be oblivious to the financial incentives which would sweep the old ones out of the ghetto. The only reasonable way for ghetto dwellers to handle this unruly situation would be to form a "shopping collective," with members helping one another in the arduous task of shopping. But to do this would be to revert to a way of life in which food gathering becomes a very time-consuming activity. Instead of developing skills as producers and pulling themselves out of poverty, ghetto dwellers would be reduced to working on collectivist schemes made necessary by the disappearance of the ghetto merchants. The proof that this is an inefficient alternative is that it is not presently used, in the face of competition from the ghetto merchant.

If this came to pass, the "progressive forces" of city planning would undoubtedly come forth with an alternative solution of letting the government take over by nationalizing the (ghetto) merchant business. The logic here defies analysis. For since it is clear that government intervention would create the chaos (by prohibiting price differentials in the ghetto) in the first place, how can the solution lie in still more government intervention?

The first problem with the suggested solution is that it is immoral. It involves forcing everyone to pay for a nationalized food industry whether or not they wish to. It also curtails the freedom of citizens by prohibiting them from entering this industry.

The second problem is pragmatic. Based on the evidence available, such a solution would be unworkable. Up to the present time, all government involvement in the economy has been marked by inefficiency, venality, and corruption, and the evidence suggests that this is not merely accidental.

The inefficiency is easy to explain, and rather widely understood. A government "enterprise" can be expected to be inefficient because it is immune to the selective process of the marketplace. In the market, the entrepreneurs who are most able to satisfy consumer desires reap the greatest profits. Obversely, the entrepreneurs who are least efficient, who provide the fewest satisfactions to consumers, suffer losses. They tend, therefore, to drop out of the market, and make it possible for those most adept at consumer satisfaction to grow and expand. This continual process of the selection of the fittest ensures the efficiency of entrepreneurs. Since the government is immune to it, it fails to regulate governmental economic activity.

The venality and corruption of the government is, if anything, even easier to see. What is difficult, however, is to realize that corruption is a *necessary* part of governmental operation of business. This is more difficult to comprehend because of our basic assumption about the motivations of those who enter government. We readily concede that people enter business in order to gain money, prestige, or power. These are basic human drives. But when it comes to government, we lose contact with this basic insight. We feel that those who enter government service are "above the fray." They are "neutral" and "objective." We may acknowledge that *some* government officials are venal, corrupt, and profit seeking, but these are considered exceptions to the rule. The *basic* motive of those in government is, we insist, selfless service to others.

It is time to challenge this erroneous concept. Individuals who enter government are no different from any other group. They are heir to *all* the temptations that flesh is heir to. We know we can assume self-seeking on the part of businessmen, unionists, and others. It can be assumed just as clearly to be operative in government officials. Not in some of them, but in *all* of them.

It is hardly necessary to point out the significance of all the government failures in the food area: agricultural subsidies, tariffs, minimum prices, maximum prices, and the "don't grow on this land" policies. Clearly, these programs are not merely inefficient attempts to provide for the public weal, although they are that. But the giveaways to big-business farmers and the payments for not growing food are also thinly disguised attempts on the part of government-bureaucrats to bilk the public.

If the government became the merchant of the ghetto, the situation would be far worse than that under private ghetto merchants. Both groups are seeking profits. The only difference is that one has the power to compel us to obey; the other does not. The government can compel our patronage; private merchants can only compete for it.

22

THE SPECULATOR

K ill the speculators! is a cry made during every famine that has ever existed. Uttered by demagogues, who think that the speculator causes death through starvation by raising food prices, this cry is fervently supported by the masses of economic illiterates. This kind of thinking, or rather nonthinking, has allowed dictators to impose even the death penalty for traders in food who charge high prices during famines. And without the feeblest of protests from those usually concerned with civil rights and liberties.

Yet the truth of the matter is that far from causing starvation and famines, it is the speculator who prevents them. And far from safeguarding the lives of the people, it is the dictator who must bear the prime responsibility for causing the famine in the first place. Thus, the popular hatred for the speculator is as great a perversion of justice as can be imagined. We can best see this by realizing that the speculator is a person who buys and sells commodities in the hope of making a profit. He is the one who, in the time-honored phrase, tries to "buy low and sell high."

But, what does buying low, selling high, and making large profits have to do with saving people from starvation? Adam

Smith explained it best with the doctrine of "the invisible hand." According to this doctrine, "every individual endeavors to employ his capital so that its produce may be of the greatest value. He generally neither intends to promote the public interest, nor knows how much he is promoting it. And he intends only his own security, his own gain. He is led in this as if by an invisible hand to promote an end which was no part of his intention. By pursuing his own interest he frequently promotes that of society more effectually than when he really intends to promote it."[1] The successful speculator, therefore, acting in his own selfish interest, neither knowing nor caring about the public good, promotes it.

First, the speculator lessens the effects of famine by storing food in times of plenty, through a motive of personal profit. He buys and stores food against the day when it might be scarce, enabling him to sell at a higher price. The consequences of his activity are far-reaching. They act as a signal to other people in the society, who are encouraged by the speculator's activity to do likewise. Consumers are encouraged to eat less and save more, importers to import more, farmers to improve their crop yields, builders to erect more storage facilities, and merchants to store more food. Thus, fulfilling the doctrine of the "invisible hand," the speculator, by his profit-seeking activity, causes more food to be stored during years of plenty than otherwise would have been the case, thereby lessening the effects of the lean years to come.

However, objections will be raised that these good consequences will follow only if the speculator is correct in his assessment of future conditions. What if he is wrong? What if he predicts years of plenty—and by selling, encourages others to do likewise—and lean years follow? In this case, wouldn't he be responsible for *increasing* the severity of the famine?

Yes. If the speculator is wrong, he would be responsible for a great deal of harm. But there are powerful forces at work which tend to eliminate incompetent speculators. Thus, the danger they

---

[1]Adam Smith, *An Inquiry into the Nature and Causes of the Wealth of Nations* (New York: Random House, 1973), p. 243, paraphrased.

*"Excellent idea, Winslow. The rich too must eat in a famine.
Along with staples we'll store up ten thousand tons of gourmet foods."*

represent and the harm they do are more theoretical than real.
The speculator who guesses wrong will suffer severe financial
losses. Buying high and selling low may misdirect the economy,
but it surely creates havoc with the speculator's pocketbook. A
speculator cannot be expected to have a perfect record of predic-
tion, but if the speculator guesses wrong more often than right,
he will tend to lose his stock of capital. Thus he will not remain
in a position where he can increase the severity of famines by his
errors. The same activity which harms the public automatically
harms the speculator, and so prevents him from continuing such

activities. Thus at any given time, existing speculators are likely to be very efficient indeed, and, therefore, beneficial to the economy.

Contrast this with the activity of governmental agencies when they assume the speculator's task of stabilizing the food market. They too try to steer a fine line between storing up too little food and storing up too much. But if they are in error, there is no weeding-out process. The salary of a government employee does not rise and fall with the success of his speculative ventures. Since it is not his own money which will be gained or lost, the care with which bureaucrats can be expected to attend to their speculations leaves much to be desired. There is no automatic, ongoing daily improvement in the accuracy of bureaucrats, as there is for private speculators.

The oft-quoted objection remains that the speculator causes food prices to rise. If his activity is carefully studied, however, it will be seen that the total effect is rather the *stabilization* of prices.

In times of plenty, when food prices are unusually low, the speculator buys. He takes some of the food off the market, thus causing prices to rise. In the lean years which follow, this stored food goes on the market, thus causing prices to fall. Of course, food will be costly during a famine, and the speculator will sell it for more than his original purchase price. But food will not be as costly as it would have been *without* his activity! (It should be remembered that the speculator does not *cause* food shortages which are usually the result of crop failures and other natural or man-made disasters.)

The effect of the speculator on food prices is to level them off. In times of plenty, when food prices are *low*, the speculator by *buying up* and storing food causes them to rise. In times of famine, when food prices are *high*, the speculator *sells off* and causes prices to fall. The effect on him is to earn profits. This is not villainous; on the contrary, the speculator performs a valuable service.

Yet instead of honoring the speculator, demagogues and their followers revile him. But prohibiting food speculation has the same effect on society as preventing squirrels from storing up nuts for winter—it leads to starvation.

23

THE IMPORTER

The International Ladies' Garment Workers' Union (ILGWU) has recently launched an unusual, extensive, and costly advertising campaign. For racist, jingoistic appeal, it is unparalleled. The theme of the campaign is that "foreigners" (dishonest and undeserving) are taking jobs away from Americans (honest, upstanding, and forthright). Perhaps the most famous ad in the series is the one which depicts an American flag above the caption "Made in Japan." Another presents a picture of a baseball glove, with the caption "The Great Un-American Game." The accompanying copy explains that baseball gloves and American flags are imported.

The *raison d'etre*, we are told, for these scathing attacks on imports is that they create unemployment in America. And on a superficial level, the argument seems plausible. After all, every American flag or baseball glove that *could* have been produced domestically, but was instead imported, represents work that could have been produced by Americans. Certainly, this means less employment for American workers than would otherwise be the case. If the argument was limited to this aspect, the ILGWU's case for the restriction, if not prohibition of imports, would be well-made.

1. The argument, however, is fallacious, and the consequences to which it logically leads are clearly unsound. The premise which justifies protectionism on the national level also justifies it on the state level. We shall ignore the political impossibility (unconstitutionality) of one state setting up tariffs between it and other states. This is, after all, irrelevant to the *economic* argument of the antifree trade ILGWU. Theoretically, any one state could justify its policy in exactly the same way that a nation can. For example, the state of Montana could bar imports from other states on the grounds that they represent labor which a Montanan could have been given but was not. A "Buy Montana" program would then be in order. It would be just as illogical and unsound as the ILGWU's "Buy American" campaign.

The argument, however, does not end at the state level. It can, with equal justification, be applied to cities. Consider the importation of a baseball glove into the city of Billings, Montana. The production of this item could have created employment for an inhabitant of Billings, but it did not. Rather, it created jobs, say, for the citizens of Roundup, Montana, where it was manufactured. The city fathers of Billings could take the ILGWU position and "patriotically" declare a moratorium on trade between the citizens of their city and the foreign economic aggressors in Roundup. This tariff, like those of the larger political subdivisions, would be designed to save the jobs of the citizens.

But there is no logical reason to halt the process at the city level. The ILGWU thesis can be logically extended to neighborhoods in Billings, or to streets within neighborhoods. "Buy Elm Street" or "Stop exporting jobs to Maple Street" could become rallying cries for the protectionists. Likewise, the inhabitants of any one block on Elm Street could turn on their neighbors on another block along the street. And even there the argument would not stop. We would have to conclude that it applies even to *individuals*. For clearly, every time an individual makes a purchase, he is forgoing the manufacture of it himself. Every time he buys shoes, a pair of pants, a baseball glove, or a flag, he is creating employment opportunities for someone else and, thereby, foreclosing those of his own. Thus the internal logic of the ILGWU's protectionist argument leads to an insistence upon absolute self-sufficiency, to a total economic interest in forgoing trade with all other people, and self-manufacture of all items necessary for well-being.

Clearly, such a view is absurd. The entire fabric of civilization rests upon mutual support, cooperation, and trade between people. To advocate the cessation of all trade is nonsense, and yet it follows ineluctably from the protectionist position. If the argument for the prohibition of trade at the national level is accepted, there is no logical stopping place at the level of the state, the city, the neighborhood, the street, or the block. The only stopping place is the individual, because the individual is the smallest possible unit. Premises which lead ineluctably to an absurd conclusion are themselves absurd. Thus, however convincing the protectionist argument might seem on the surface, there is *something* terribly wrong with it.

Specifically, the essence of the fallacy is a misunderstanding of the nature and function of free trade. Trade, we believe, outstrips fire, the wheel, and the opposable thumb in explaining man's superiority over the animals. For it and it alone makes specialization and the division of labor possible.

In their daily lives people consume virtually hundreds of thousands of different items every year. If not for specialization, each person would be forced to manufacture these items by himself. This would be an impossible task. As a matter of fact, people would not even be able to produce enough food for themselves, let alone produce all other goods which they might desire. *Efficient* production of food involves the production of many other things, including capital equipment. The production of these things would involve *every person* in the manufacture of all the items that are now distributed over an entire population. It is quite true that without fire, the wheel, and opposable thumbs, mankind would find itself in a sorry state indeed. But without specialization, since it would be impossible for virtually anyone to even feed himself, everyone would be faced with the prospect of starvation and death.

With specialization, each person can limit his productive efforts to those areas he performs best in. But trade is the linch-pin that holds this system together. Without the possibility of trade, people would amass enormous quantities of unusable safety pins, paper clips, or whatever. Without the possibility of trade, the incentive for specialization and the division of labor would be gone. Everyone would be forced back into the suicidal attempt to become self-sufficient.

2. Another significant reason for rejecting the protectionist argument is that it fails to take exports into account. It is true that for every American flag or baseball glove imported into this country, some domestic jobs are lost. But what the protectionists conveniently forget is that for every job lost in a domestic indus-try because of competition with imports, a job can be gained in an export industry.

Let us assume that the states of Vermont and Florida are self-sufficient. Both produce, among other things, maple syrup and oranges. Because of the differing climatic conditions, maple syrup is scarce and expensive in Florida, and oranges are scarce and expensive in Vermont. Vermont oranges have to be grown in greenhouses, and Florida maple syrup comes from maple trees grown in large refrigerators.

What would happen if trade were suddenly begun between the two states? Vermont would of course begin to import oranges and Florida would import maple syrup. Were the ILGWU, or any other protectionist pressure group on the scene, it would quickly point out that importing maple syrup into Florida would ruin that state's small maple syrup industry, and the importation of oranges into Vermont would ruin the orange industry there. The protectionists would ignore the fact that jobs would be gained in Florida in the orange industry, and in Ver-mont, in the maple syrup industry. They would focus our atten-tion on the jobs *lost* due to *imports* and would completely ignore the jobs *gained* because of *exports*. It is, of course, true that jobs will be lost in Vermont in the orange industry and in the maple syrup industry in Florida. But it is no less true that jobs will *increase* in the maple syrup industry of Vermont and in the orange industry in Florida.

There may well be fewer jobs available in both industries in both states since orange growing can be done with less manpower in Florida than in Vermont, and maple syrup can be manufactured more efficiently in Vermont than in Florida. But far from being a bad effect, this is one of the *gains* of trade! The workers freed from these industries become available for projects that could not be undertaken before. For example, if a modern system of transportation did not exist, and industry had to rely on individuals carrying 100 pound loads on their backs, hundreds and thousands of people would have to be withdrawn from other fields to fill the needs of the transport industry. Thus, many projects and industries would have to be abandoned. With modern methods, fewer workers are needed. The extra workers are thus free to move into other areas, with all the consequent benefits to society.

Whether or not there will be fewer jobs in the orange and maple syrup industries in Vermont and Florida in the final analysis depends upon the way the people wish to spend their newfound income. It is only if these people decide to spend all the newfound income on extra oranges and maple syrup that the total employment in these two industries will not change after trade begins. Then the same number of workers will produce more maple syrup and oranges. More likely, though, the people will decide to spend some of their newfound income in these two goods, and the rest on other goods. In that case, employment in these two areas will decrease somewhat (although this decreased workforce may still be able to produce more than before), but employment will increase in the industries whose products are most wanted by the consumers.

Viewed in its totality then, the opening of trade between the two regions benefits both of them. Although employment will fall in the industries supplanted by imports, it will rise in export industries and in the new industries developing because of the availability of workers. But the protectionists are not entirely wrong. Trade does create problems in the industries supplanted and some workers will suffer in the short run. There will, for example, no longer be a brisk demand for Vermonters who specialize in the production of oranges, or for Floridians who produce maple syrup. There will be jobs for these people in other industries, but since they will have to enter these fields as beginners, they will probably have to accept a salary cut. They may also need considerable retraining.

So the question arises: Who is to pay for the retraining, and who is to bear the loss associated with the lower salaries in the new industry? The protectionists, of course, would advocate that the government or the capitalists should pick up the tab. But this is not justified.

First, it should be noted that only *skilled* workers face a cut in wages because of a move to a new industry. The others will enter the new industry on much the same level as that in which they functioned in the old. Instead of sweeping the floors of a maple syrup plant, they will sweep the floors of perhaps a textile factory. The skilled worker, by contrast, has specific skills which are of greater use in one industry than in another. He is not equally useful in the new industry, and cannot command the same salary.

Second, it should be understood that the skilled worker is an investor, just as the capitalist. The capitalist invests in material things, and the worker invests in his skills. All investors have one thing in common, and that is that the returns on their investment are uncertain. In fact, the greater the risk involved, the more the investor may gain. In the example given, part of the reason skilled orange growers in Vermont and skilled maple syrup producers in Florida were earning high salaries, before the advent of trade between the states, was the risk that some day such trade might begin.

Should the skilled orange growers, now that they must leave the industry in which they were highly paid specialists, be subsidized for retraining and for the salary cuts they must accept in the interim? Or should they bear the expenses and losses themselves? It seems clear that any subsidy would be an attempt to maintain the skilled worker in the style to which he had become accustomed, without asking him to bear any of the risk that made such a high standard of living possible in the first place. In addition, such a subsidy, coming out of tax revenues which are paid mainly by the poor, would constitute a forced subsidy to rich skilled workers from poor, unskilled workers.

3. Now consider a situation which, on the surface, seems to be the protectionist's nightmare come true. Imagine that there is one country which can outproduce the others in *all* industries. Suppose Japan (the ILGWU's bugaboo), can produce *everything* more efficiently than America—not only flags, baseball gloves, radios, televisions, cars, and tape recorders, but *everything*. Would the ILGWU's contention that we should forcibly restrict trade be valid then?

The answer is that it is *never* justifiable to restrict trade between two consenting adults, or even nations of consenting adults, certainly not on the ground that the trade will harm one of them. For if one party to the trade thought it was harmful, he would simply refuse it. Prohibition would not be needed. And if both parties consent to the trade, what right would any third party have to prohibit it? Prohibition would be tantamount to a denial of the adulthood of one or both of the trading parties, by treating them as juveniles who did not have the sense or the right to enter into contractual obligations.

In spite of all such moral arguments, the protectionists would still want to prohibit trade on the grounds that a disaster would follow if it were not done. Let us trace the situation which would exist between the United States and Japan under the nightmare conditions that have been stipulated. Supposedly, Japan would export goods and services without importing anything from the United States. This would bring prosperity to Japanese industry, and depression to our own. Eventually, Japan would supply *all* our needs and, as there would be no exports to counterbalance this, American industry would come to a grinding halt. Unemployment would rise to epidemic proportions and there would be a complete dependency on Japan.

This description may sound a bit absurd, yet the history of protectionism in the United States, and the success of the ILGWU campaign, indicate that such "nightmares" have more currency than might be imagined. Perhaps this horrid dream prevails because it is easier to shrink back in horror from it than to confront it head-on.

In contemplating this nightmare, the question arises as to what the Americans will use to *buy* the Japanese goods with. They cannot use gold (or any of the other precious monetary metals), because gold is itself a commodity. If Americans used gold to pay for the imports they would in effect be *exporting* gold. This would counter the loss of jobs due to imports, and we would be back to the prototypical situation. Americans might lose jobs in radio and television, but gain them in gold mining. The American economy would resemble that of South Africa, which pays for its imports largely with exports of gold.

The only other means of payment would be in the form of United States dollars. But what would the Japanese do with dollars? There are only three possibilities: they could return these dollars to us as payment for our exports to them, they could keep these dollars, or they could spend them on the produce of countries other than the United States. If they opted for the last alternative, the countries with whom they traded would have the same three options: spending in the United States, hoarding, or spending in other countries, and so on for the countries these nations trade with in turn. If we divide the world into two parts—the United States and all the other countries, we can see that the three possibilities reduce to two: either the paper money we send out comes back to buy our goods or it does not.

Assume that the "worst" possibility happens—that none of the money comes back to stimulate our exports. Far from being a disaster, as the protectionists allege, this would actually be an unmitigated blessing! The paper dollars we would be sending abroad would be just that, paper, worthless paper. And we would not even have to "waste" much paper—we could simply print dollars with extra zeroes added on. So, in this ILGWU nightmare, Japan would be sending us the products of their industry, and we would be sending Japan nothing but pieces of green paper with many zeroes printed on them. It would be a prime example of a giveaway. The refusal of foreigners to cash in their dollars would amount to a large gift to the United States. We would receive the products, and they would receive worthless paper!

Contrary to the fantasies of the ILGWU and other protectionist groups, the recipients of large gifts do not usually suffer untold agonies. Israel has received reparations from Germany for many years, and gifts from the United States, without any obvious deleterious effects. The recipient country does not *have* to discontinue its own production. For the desires of any populace are infinite. If the Japanese gave a Toyota car to every individual in the United States, they would soon want two, three, or many Toyotas. Clearly, it is inconceivable for the Japanese (or anyone else) to be so self-sacrificing as to even try to satiate all the desires of the American people without recompense. Yet only if they succeeded in this impossible task would domestic industries collapse, because then *everyone* would have all he wanted of *everything*.

But in this imaginary case, the collapse of domestic industry would be something to be *praised*, not condemned. People in the United States would discontinue all production only if they felt they had enough material possessions and would continue to have enough in the future. Such a situation is not only not horrible, it would be welcomed by Americans as the closest thing to a Utopia.

In reality, of course, the Japanese and others would *not* be content to pile up the dollars we gave them as payment for their products. As soon as their dollar balances went above the level they chose, they would turn the dollars in, thereby stimulating export manufacturing in the United States. They might buy American goods, and thus directly stimulate American exports. Or they might demand gold for their dollars ("attack" the dollar), necessitating a devaluation which would make American exports more competitive in the world markets. Either way, the dollars would come back to the United States, and our domestic export industries would be stimulated. The employment lost due to imports would be countered by increases elsewhere, just as in the Vermont-Florida case.

Why would the Japanese trade with a country whose manufacturing was less efficient than their own? Because of the difference between what is called absolute advantage and comparative advantage. Trade takes place between two parties (countries, states, cities, towns, neighborhoods, streets, persons) not in accordance with their absolute ability to produce, but in accordance with their relative ability. The classical example is that of the best lawyer in town who is also the best typist. This person has an absolute advantage over his secretary in the provision of both legal and typing services. Nevertheless, the lawyer decides to specialize in the profession in which he has a *comparative advantage*—the law. For suppose he is 100 times as good a lawyer as his secretary, but only twice as efficient a typist. It is more advantageous for him to pursue the legal profession, and to hire (trade with) a typist. The secretary has a comparative advantage in typing: she has only 1 percent of the effectiveness in law, compared to her employer, but she is fully one half as good as he is typing. She is able to earn a living through trade even though she is poorer at both skills.

The Japan we have been imagining has an absolute advantage in the production of all goods. But when the Japanese return our dollars to us in return for our goods, America will export the goods in which *it* has a comparative advantage. If we are half as good as the Japanese in the production of wheat, but only one quarter as good in the production of radios, we will export wheat in payment for our importation of radios. And we will all gain.

Thus, no matter what situation is envisioned—even the most extreme—the protectionist argument proves inadequate. But because of the emotional potency of its appeal, importers have long been vilified. For their persistence in a task which is inherently helpful, importers should be looked upon as the great benefactors they are.

24

THE MIDDLEMAN

We are told that middlemen are exploitative. Even worse than other profiteers—who at least provide some type of service—the middleman is considered entirely unproductive. He buys a product which someone else has made, and resells it at a higher price, having added nothing whatsoever to it, except the cost to the consumer. If there were no middlemen, goods and services would be cheaper, with no reduction in quantity or quality.

Although this concept is popular and prevalent, it is an incorrect one. It reveals a shocking ignorance of the economic function of middlemen, who do indeed perform a service. If they were eliminated, the whole order of production would be thrown into chaos. Goods and services would be in short supply, if they were available at all, and the money that would have to be spent to obtain them would rise wildly.

The production process of a typical "commodity" consists of raw materials which must be gathered and worked on. Machinery and other factors used in production must be obtained, set up, repaired, etc. When the final product emerges, it must be insured, transported, and kept track of. It must be advertised and retailed. Records must be kept, legal work must be done, and the finances must be in good order.

Production and consumption of our typical commodity
could be portrayed in the following manner:

No. 10
9
8
7
6
5
4
3
2
1

Number 10 represents the first stage in the production of our
commodity and no. 1 the last stage when the commodity is in
the hands of the consumer. Stages no. 2 through no. 9 indicate
the intermediate stages of production. All of these are handled
by middlemen. For example, no. 4 may be an advertiser, a
retailer, wholesaler, jobber, agent, intermediary, financier,
assembler, or shipper. No matter what his specific title or function, this middleman buys from no. 5 and resells the product to
no. 3. Without specifying, or even knowing exactly what he
does, it is obvious that the middleman performs a necessary
service in an efficient manner.

If it were not a necessary service, no. 3 would not buy the
product from no. 4 at a higher price than that at which he could
buy the product from no. 5. If no. 4 were not performing a valuable service, no. 3 would "cut out the middleman" and buy the
product directly from no. 5.

So it is apparent that no. 4 is doing an efficient job—at least
a more efficient job than no. 3 could do himself. If he were not,
no. 3 would again cut out middleman no. 4, and do the job himself.

It is also true that no. 4, although performing a necessary
function in an efficient manner, does not overcharge for his
efforts. If he did, it would pay for no. 3 to circumvent him, and

either take on the task himself, or subcontract it to another middleman. In addition, if no. 4 were earning a higher profit than that earned in the other stages of production, entrepreneurs in the other stages would tend to move into this stage, and drive down the rate of profit until it was equivalent to the profit earned at the other stages (with given risk and uncertainty).

If the no. 4 middleman were eliminated by a legal decree, his job would have to be taken over by the no. 3s, no. 5s, or others, or they would not get done at all. If the no. 3s, or the no. 5s took over the job, the cost of production would rise. The fact that they dealt with no. 4 as long as it was legally possible to do so indicates that they cannot do the job as well—that is, for the same price or less. If the no. 4 stage were completely eliminated, and nobody took over this function, then the process of production would be seriously disrupted at this point.

The present analysis notwithstanding, many people will continue to think that there is something more "pure" and "direct" in exchanges which do not involve a middleman. Perhaps the problems involved with what economists call the "double coincidence of wants" will disabuse them of this view.

Consider the plight of the person who has in his possession a barrel of pickles which he would like to trade for a chicken. He must find someone who has a chicken and would like to trade it for a barrel of pickles. Imagine how rare a coincidence would have to occur for the desires of each of these people to be met. Such a "double coincidence of wants" is so rare, in fact, that both people would naturally gravitate toward an intermediary, if one were available. For example, the chicken-wanting pickle owner could trade his wares to the middleman for a more marketable commodity (gold) and then use the gold to buy a chicken. If he did, it would no longer be necessary for him to find a chicken-owning pickle wanter. Any chicken owner will do, whether he wants pickles or not. Obviously, the trade is vastly simplified by the advent of the middleman. He *makes a double coincidence of wants unnecessary*. Far from preying on the consumer, it is the middleman who in many instances makes the trade the consumer wishes possible.

Some attacks on the middleman are based on arguments which are represented in the following diagrams. In an earlier time, represented by diagram 1, the price of the good was low, and the share that went to the middleman was low. Then (diagram 2), the share of the value of the final good that went to the middleman rose, and so did the cost of the good. Examples such as these were used to prove that the high prices of meat in the spring of 1973 were due to middlemen. But they prove, if anything, quite the opposite. The share going to the middlemen may have risen, but only because the contributions made by middlemen have also increased! An increased share without an increased contribution would simply raise profits and attract

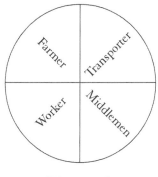

Diagram 1

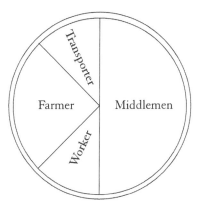

Diagram 2

many more entrepreneurs to the area. And their entry would dissipate the profits. So if the share which goes to middlemen rises, it must be because of their productivity.

Examples of this phenomenon abound in the annals of business economics. Who can deny that department stores and supermarkets play a greater role (and take a greater share of the market) than middlemen in times past? Yet department stores and supermarkets lead to *more* efficiency, and *lower* prices. These new modes of retailing necessitate *more* expenditures on the middleman phases of production, but greater efficiency leads to lower prices.

25

THE PROFITEER

It is clear that profits and everything associated with them have been under attack for a long time. What is not so clear is the reason for these attacks.

Several different patterns can be discerned. The objection most often made is that profits, unlike other sources of income such as wages, rents, or even interest (payment for waiting risk), are *unearned*. There is no honest labor or effort associated with profit making to justify the benefits. Most people do not understand the process by which profits are attained, and assume there is *something* untoward going on. . . . "It isn't fair to make profits without having to *work* for them."

Another objection often voiced against profits, and especially against profiteering (unreasonable profits), is that such profits impoverish the rest of mankind. The notion is that there is only a finite amount of wealth available and if the profiteers get more of it, there is less for everyone else. Thus, not only are profits "undeserved" because they are "unearned," but they actually harm people by diverting funds from the rest of society.

It also appears to many that profits are earned by taking advantage of the helplessness of others. This view constitutes a third type of objection, and is reflected in the scornful popular expression that profiteers earn their income "from the misery of others." When the "helplessness" consists of a lack of knowledge, the critics of profits are especially vociferous in their condemnation. For example, the case where a profit is earned solely because the customer is unaware that the same commodity is being sold close by at a lower price, is particularly vexing. When the customer is poor, the profiteer is even more condemned.

The usual defenses of the idea and practice of earning a profit leave a great deal to be desired. They have in the past been limited to pointing out: (1) profits are patriotic, and that to attack them is un-American or perhaps communistic; (2) they are not very big, anyway; and (3) they are used, in many cases, for charitable contributions. Needless to say, these are not very formidable defenses. Consideration must be given to the function of profits in a modern economy, and an effort made to provide a somewhat more spirited defense for the ancient and honorable vocation of profiteering.

First, profits are earned by entrepreneurs who see and seize upon opportunities which are not readily apparent to other people. The opportunity grasped by the entrepreneur may vary from case to case, but in all cases people are offered trades which they hold to be in their advantage, and which would not be offered in the absence of the entrepreneur. In the most usual case, the entrepreneur sees a discrepancy between different prices—strawberries selling at 25¢ per jar in New Jersey, and 45¢ in New York. As long as the costs associated with the transport of strawberries (transportation, insurance, storage, breakage, spoilage, etc.) are less than the price differential of 20¢ per jar, the enterprising entrepreneur is in a position to offer two sets of trades. He can offer to buy strawberries in New Jersey at a price slightly higher than the prevailing 25¢ per jar, and then offer to sell strawberries to New Yorkers at a price below the 45¢ per jar that prevails in that market. In both cases, if he finds any takers, he will benefit those he deals with, either by offering a higher price for their goods than they have been accustomed to receiving, or by offering to sell them goods at a lower price than they are accustomed to paying.

In addition to the intratemporal price discrepancy case, there is the intertemporal case, where a price discrepancy between present goods and future goods is perceived. Take frisbees as an example. Consider all the factors of production—land, labor, and capital—which are embodied in the final good of the frisbees offered for sale. The factors of production are goods of a sort themselves, and, therefore, have prices attached to them. After taking due account of the time it will take to convert these factors into the final good, three possibilities emerge: (1) there is no price discrepancy between the prices of the factors and the price of the future good; (2) there is a discrepancy, and the factor prices are high, relative to the price of the good; and (3) there is a discrepancy, and the price of the final good is high relative to the prices of the factors.

If there is no price discrepancy, the successful entrepreneur will not act. But if the factor prices are relatively high, the entrepreneur will withdraw from production. It would be wasteful to devote relatively valuable resources on a final good that will be relatively valueless. He might sell his shares in the companies which engage in such production. Or, if he does not hold shares, he can contract to sell them in the future at their present high price (which does not yet reflect the production error of manufacturing frisbees with resources that are more valuable than the frisbees themselves will be). He can cover these sales by purchases of the same amount of shares in the future, when he expects their value to be lower, because of the production error. There are many people who are mystified by this process, often called "selling short." They wonder how it is possible to sell something that you do not own, in the future, but at today's prices. Strictly speaking, one cannot sell anything that one does not own. But it is certainly possible to *promise* to sell something in the future that one does not yet own, on the understanding that one can always *buy* it in the future, and *then* deliver it, in fulfillment of the sales contract. In order to test the understanding of this concept, we can ask who would agree to *buy* shares in the future at the present price? People who expect the price to rise even further, but do not want to invest their money now.

If, on the other hand, the entrepreneur thinks that the price of the final good is likely to be greater than the combined costs of all the factors, he will engage in the opposite behavior. He will produce the frisbees and/or invest in companies which undertake such production.

The third type of hidden opportunity which the entrepreneur can seize upon does not involve any price discrepancies, either inter- or intratemporal. This type of opportunity involves goods that have not yet been produced, and therefore have no prices at all. Consider in this regard the frisbee *before* it was produced or invented. There was no guarantee, at that time, that the public would accept it. In cases of this kind, the entrepreneur feels, thinks, or divines that there is something, the lack of which may not even be apparent to anyone else, that consumers would greatly value if they could but be told of its existence and convinced of its beneficial attributes. In this case the entrepreneur plays nursemaid to the idea, through the processes of invention, financing, advertising, and all other steps necessary to bring an idea to public acceptance.

After having considered some of the types of activities profit making entrepreneurs are likely to engage in, the results of profit seeking can be assessed.

One result is immediately apparent—the collection and dissemination of knowledge. The knowledge of hitherto unproduced products is an obvious and dramatic example, but as we have seen, the knowledge engendered by profit seeking behavior is by no means limited to such exotic occurrences. On a daily basis, the profit seeker is constantly bringing to the market knowledge about price differentials, both inter- and intratemporal.

This knowledge is of great benefit to all concerned. Without it, people in New Jersey would be eating strawberries which they would much rather sell, if they could find someone willing to pay more than 25¢ per jar. That is, the New Jerseyans only eat the berries because of their lack of knowledge of people who value them more than they themselves. In addition, without this knowledge, there would be people in New York *not* eating strawberries because they assume that the only way to get them is to pay 45¢ a jar, when in truth, they could be had for less.

Of course, the profit seeker does not bring this knowledge to bear as a *teacher* might. He is not one who goes about the countryside explicitly imparting information. As a matter of fact, after his work is done, none of the people in New Jersey and New York may even be aware of the relative prices of strawberries in those markets. What the profit seeker does is make sure that the *effects* of knowledge of prices in the different areas are felt. The profit seeker does not directly spread the knowledge himself; he merely spreads the strawberries which, in the absence of knowledge of their prices, would not have been so allocated.

It is perfectly true then, that the profit maker takes advantage of the ignorance of other people. If the relevant knowledge were present, the entrepreneur could hardly earn profits by shipping strawberries from New Jersey to New York. Although true, however, it is hardly reprehensible. Anyone whose function it is to sell a commodity *must* sell it to those who lack it. The fact that the lack is determined by ignorance does not make the lack—or the need—any less real. The profit seeker "takes advantage" of the lack of knowledge of his customers in the same way that the farmer "takes advantage" of the hunger of his customer—by providing that which his customer lacks.

The profits of the entrepreneur, therefore, are not made at the expense of anyone else. It is not true that there must be losses elsewhere in the economy equal to the gains of the entrepreneur, because it is not true that the entrepreneur fails to create anything. The entrepreneur does create. He creates the possibility of cooperation between disparate, and in many cases widely separated, groups. He is a broker or intermediary in *opportunities*, as it were. It is his function to see to it that mutually beneficial opportunities are not bypassed. Why this type of effort should be singled out and denigrated as "not honest work" is beyond the scope of reason.

In addition to serving as a focal point for the utilization of knowledge, the profit seeking entrepreneur benefits people by offering them choices otherwise not open to them. The case in

"Ah! I suspected as much. He's a masochist!"

which the entrepreneur presents the public with an entirely new product is again an obvious example. But the principle has applications even in the more mundane case of intertemporal price discrepancies. For society benefits when valuable resources are *not* committed to final products which are less valuable than the resources themselves. Such resources can be used in the production of more valuable final products, that is to say, in the production of final products which consumers value more.

It should be borne in mind that all entrepreneurial transactions are strictly voluntary. The people with whom the entrepreneur deals are just as free to reject as to accept his offers. If they accept, therefore, it can only be because they feel that they benefit from trading with him. They may rue their decision, and wish they had made their purchase at a lower price, or sold their goods at a higher price. But this does not alter the claim that the profit seeking entrepreneur offers a trade which, at the time it is offered, is considered beneficial by all the parties to it. This is an important claim, and it speaks well for the entrepreneur. It is a claim which cannot, for example, be made on behalf of government transactions because they cannot be said to be fully voluntary.

Another result of the profit making process is that after it is undergone in any given market, there is less scope for its continuation. Its success sows the seeds for its demise. Once the opportunity has been pointed out and fulfilled by the entrepreneur, his function is completed. Like the Lone Ranger of a bygone era, the "lone entrepreneur" must move on to make other pastures greener. However, if imbalances in prices should arise shortly thereafter, the profit seeker will return.

The incentive behind the entrepreneur's attempt to hold together the disparate parts of the economy is, of course, the profits he hopes to gain thereby. This is an excellent example of the beneficial effects of a profit and loss system. For the successful entrepreneur—the one who earns profits—holds the economy together by decreasing price discrepancies. But the entrepreneur who buys when he should sell, or sells when he should buy (who instead of decreasing price discrepancies and holding the economy together, increases them and disrupts the economy), loses money. The more mistakes he makes, the less able he is to continue in his error. We cannot hope to completely rid the economy of errors. But a mechanism that automatically tends to improve the performance of the entrepreneurial class at every given instant is not to be dismissed lightly.

Although a case has been made for the beneficial effects of profits, profiteering has not been mentioned. It is important to do so, for there are many who would contend, in the spirit of the Aristotelian "golden mean," that profits in moderation are acceptable, perhaps even beneficial, but that the extremism of profiteering can only be deleterious.

The word "profiteering" has always been used in a smear context. "Profits" plus "I hate the son of a bitch" equals "profiteering" in the same way that "firmness" plus "I think he is wrong" equals "stubbornness." (Bertrand Russell has said, to illustrate this point, "I'm firm, you're stubborn, and he's a pig-headed son of a bitch.") We do not have an equivalent term of opprobrium for the wage earner (wageer?) who seeks "exorbitant" or "unconscionable" wage rates. Perhaps because "public opinion" (the mass media establishment) favors high wages but not high profits.

Semantics aside, it would appear that if profits are a benefit to our society, then profiteering is of even greater benefit. The possibility of profits, as has been demonstrated, is a sign that something is amiss in the economy, indicating that people are not taking advantage of mutually beneficial trades. The actualization of profits indicates that something is being done about these missed opportunities (entrepreneurs are seeing to it that "the strawberries get properly spread around." But if the possibility of profits indicates something amiss, then the possibility of profiteering signifies even greater gaps in the economic fabric. And if mere profits indicate an economic cure in progress, then profiteering is a sign that something of a substantial magnitude is operating to rectify the situation. Instead of moderate profits being acceptable, and profiteering being "exploitative," we can see that the greater the profits, and the greater the profiteering, the better off the economy is. A medical analogy comes to mind: If Band-Aids are "good" because the body can be cared for by them, then surgery ("profiteering") is better, because it shows that a much more needy patient is being cared for.

The most important defense of profit making is based on political freedom:

There are basically only two ways to run an economy. The first, voluntaristically, with decentralism and reliance on the price and profit-and-loss system to provide information and incentive. The second, compulsorily, with central planning, economic orders and directives, reliance on the initiative of the economic dictators, and the obedience of everyone else. These two systems are the two polar extremes. All other economic systems are permutations and combinations of these two "pure" types.

The compulsory or command economy is simplicity itself in outlook. The economic leaders simply decide what is to be produced, who is to produce it and how, and who is to reap the benefits of such production.

By contrast, the voluntary or free market economy is quite complex. The individual must decide what to produce and how to produce it. The incentive is his own enjoyment of the product and what he may get for it by trading it with other people. Instead of being coordinated by economic directives, the free-market economy, as we have seen, is coordinated by the profit-and-loss mechanism.

Now consider this paradox: Those who are frequently the most virulent critics of "profiteers" and, by extension, of the whole free market system, are frequently also vociferous champions of decentralism and the rights of the individual in personal matters. Yet, insofar as they attack "profits" and "profiteering," they are attacking not only the right of individuals to function freely in the economic domain, but the very foundation for freedom in every other area of human life.

In their attacks on profits and profiteering—indeed on all things "profitable"—they show themselves to be in league with despots and dictators.

If they were to have their way, and profits were severely restricted or outlawed entirely, coercive collectivism would be to that degree strengthened. Personal liberties would be washed away in a tide of orders from the top. The individual cannot be

free if his economic existence is based on the decree of an economic dictator from whose dictates there is no appeal. In a free
market, if you quit your job, an employee leaves your service, a
customer refuses to buy from you, or a supplier refuses to sell to
you, there are other actual or potential bosses, employees, customers or suppliers. But in a controlled economy, there are no
other alternatives. Deviations, eccentricities or nonorthodox
inclinations are not tolerated.

The champions of civil liberties have a uniquely brilliant
insight, and a truly humane dictum which they apply assidu-
ously in the area of sexual morality—"Anything goes between
consenting adults, and (implicitly), nothing goes but that which
is between consenting adults." But they steadfastly refuse to
apply this rule to any area other than that of sexual morality!
Specifically, they refuse to apply it to the economic arena. But
this humane dictum should be applied to *all* parts of human life,
including the profiteer *as well as* the sexual pervert or deviant; to
the entrepreneur *as well as* the fetishist; to the speculator *as well
as* the sado-masochist.

To argue that perverts, deviants, and others of this ilk have
been unjustly denigrated is one of the main burdens of this
book. We cannot, therefore, be accused of having played fast and
loose with the deviant community. But it is *just as* unfair to treat
members of the profiteering community as pariahs.

One last criticism of profiteering and the free market is the
view that in the distant past, when there was an agrarian economy and "life was simpler," perhaps a free enterprise system was
viable. Today, what might have been appropriate for farmers and
small tradesmen simply will not do. In our complex industrial
society, we cannot afford to leave things to the anachronistic
whims of individuals. We need the strong central control of an
economic planning board, and the elimination of profits and
profiteering from our transactions.

This view is widespread. In some circles it is thought to be
"self-evident." But the analysis of profits as intimately tied up
with a lack of knowledge must lead to the opposite view. The
institution of profits is an invaluable aid in the gathering and

dissemination of knowledge and the effects of knowledge. If anything can be taken as a mark of "a highly complex modern, nonagrarian economy," it is this selfsame *lack* of economic knowledge and the utilization of it. It would, therefore, seem to follow that the profit system becomes *more* valuable as the economy becomes more complex! For in such an economy, the information provided by the automatic price and profit and loss system is essential. Economic dictatorship, if it is ever viable, which it is not, is so only in a simple economy, one which can be easily managed by one group of bureaucrats.

In conclusion, a sharp, rigid, and basic distinction must be drawn between the profits that can be earned in the marketplace, and the profits that can be "earned" through government subsidies and influence, in short, through the system of corporate-state capitalism. In the marketplace, all transfers of funds must be voluntary. Therefore, all profits must be based on the voluntary choices of the economic actors, and must hence be indicative of, and bring about solutions for, the wants of the economy. Thus, the assertion that the possibility of profits shows the scope of unrequited trades and that the actual earning of profits indicates that these gaps are being filled, applies only to the free-market economy.

These assertions cannot be made in the absence of the free market. Profits in the "mixed" economy (an economy that has elements of the free market as well as elements of coercion) might well be due to no more than the prohibition of competition. For example, a tariff on imports will increase the demand for the domestic product, and profits in the domestic industry will rise. But it can hardly be concluded from this that any new information was uncovered, or that consumer satisfaction was in any way increased. If anything, the opposite would be the case. The tie between profits and well-being is thus sundered and we can no longer infer the latter from the former.

VII. Ecology

26

THE STRIPMINER

There are basically two methods of mining coal: strip mining and deep mining. In deep mining, an intricate set of tunnels, shafts, and braces are set deep in the earth. People who work in such mines for long periods of time commonly contract "black lung disease," the dreaded miner's malady caused by breathing in coal particles. Deep mining is hazardous to workers in other ways. Mine entrapments, for example, in which hundreds of miners are trapped far below the surface of the earth, occur with deadly regularity. The immediate cause may be a cave-in, escaping gas, an explosion, or water seepage, but the ultimate cause is the deep-mining method itself.

In strip mining, as the name implies, the earth is stripped, layer by layer, until the coal stream is unearthed. Although especially well suited for coal beds that lie close to the surface, strip mining has also proven feasible at moderate depths. Strip mining is free of the danger of cave-ins, and other forms of entrapment, and of black lung disease. It is also a much cheaper method than deep mining. In spite of these advantages, strip mining has been roundly condemned by practically all sources of "informed," "liberal," and "progressive" opinion.

The supposed explanation for this otherwise inexplicable state of affairs centers around two criticisms of strip mining: it is said to cause pollution, and to despoil the natural beauty of the landscape. But as can be seen from even a cursory examination, these criticisms hardly suffice. Even if they were correct, it would be difficult to reconcile humanistic impulses with a preference for deep mining. For there is no black lung disease among miners who work on the surface of the earth; there is no danger of cave-ins or entrapment. Clearly, life is on the side of strip mining.

But, upon examination, it is clear that the criticism is by no means correct. First consider pollution. Although it is true that pollution does in fact result from strip mining, it is not a *necessary* concomitant. It can be eliminated, and it would be eliminated, if laws prohibiting trespass were enforced.

What is presently done during the strip mining of coal is to pile up in high mounds the earth that must be peeled away to expose the coal. These mounds are usually piled near streams of water. Substantial amounts are borne away by the streams, contaminating them and the lakes and waterways into which they feed. Also, the denuded land becomes a source of mudslides; thus, as a result of what the strip miner does, the whole environment is damaged.

But these are not necessary elements of the strip mining process. Although a person may do whatever he wishes with land that he owns, if what he does damages land belonging to others, he should be made to bear the costs of the damage. If, for example, the strip miner's activities result in mudslides and destruction of other people's land and goods, he is liable. Part of his responsibility may be to reseed or otherwise rehabilitate the land to eliminate the possibility of future mudslides. If strip miners were made to bear the full costs of their activity, and if the property owners downstream were granted preventative injunctions if they were unwilling to be compensated for damages, then the pollution would cease.

It is most important to see that the present link between pollution and strip mining has no inherent status, but is rather entirely due to the failure to apply the common laws of trespass against the strip miners. Imagine any other industry, such as the

hula hoop industry, that was allowed to violate the law in this manner. Now there is no *necessary* connection between the hula hoop industry and pollution. But if excess plastic clutter were *allowed*, there soon would be a connection between this industry and pollution, at least in the mind of the public. And so it is with the coal mining industry, and with strip mining in particular. There is nothing about the strip mining method of coal mining that is inherently pollution-causing. It is only because the laws of trespass have not been rigidly applied to the strip miners that the link between stripping and pollution exists. Let these laws be fully adhered to and this argument against strip mining will disappear.

What of the other argument against the strip miner: that stripping spoils the natural beauty of the landscape? This is a shaky objection at best because, when it comes to beauty or aesthetics, there are no objective standards. What is beautiful to one person may be ugly to another and vice versa. It is true that strip mining removes the vegetation, grass, and trees from the landscape. It can turn a lush, fertile landscape into a veritable desert. But some people prefer the desolation and emptiness of the desert! The Painted Desert in Arizona, the salt flats of Utah, and the Grand Canyon of Colorado are considered by many people to be places of great beauty.

If contrast is one of the concomitants of natural beauty, then the small bits of barren land created by strip miners amidst the lush greenery of the Appalachians actually add to the beauty of the scene. Certainly we cannot unambiguously and objectively fault the strip miner on the grounds that he destroys the beauty of the landscape.

But discussions about aesthetic criteria will not resolve the issue raised by the critics, since the issue is not really about beauty, though it is phrased as if it were. The real objection seems to be that strip mining is an intrusion upon nature by an offensive industrial society. The notion that land areas should be left in their "natural state" seems to be the operative one. But if the lovers and protectors of "nature as-is" have the right to prevent strip miners from operating, then they also have the right to prevent farmers from clearing virgin soil and planting upon it, and to prevent builders from erecting buildings, bridges, factories, airports, and hospitals. The "argument from nature" is really an argument against civilization and against the use of human intelligence.

Actually, many among those who condemn strip mining as "unnatural" would themselves object vigorously if other

conditions—homosexuality or miscegenation, for example—
were objected to on those grounds. They would point out very
little is "natural" to man, and that sometimes what is natural—
murderous rage, for example—is not what is best. Civilization
depends to a great extent upon our being able to transcend
nature.

To say of a thing that it is "natural" or "unnatural" is not to
say anything about that thing's intrinsic value. A thing's value
depends upon whether or not it satisfies our needs, and contributes to our well-being. Strip mining, when evaluated ration-
ally, fulfills these more rational criteria.

27

THE LITTERER

The litterer today will find few defenders. He is beset on all sides, bearing the brunt of the barbs of do-gooder groups. Radio and television stations beam anti-litter messages as a "public service," neighborhood and parent-teacher associations, church groups, and civic organizations are in agreement on the issue of littering. The film industry, which must pass over many topics as too controversial, is united in its hatred for litter. Litter is a great unifier.

There is, however, one small, seemingly insignificant detail which destroys the case against litter and the litterer. Litter can *only* take place in the public domain, *never* in the private domain. The ads showing the supposed evils of litter take place on highways, beaches, streets, parks, subways, or public bath-rooms—all *public* areas. This is not because *most* littering occurs in public places. It is definitional. If something resembling litter-ing in *all* other aspects were to occur in a private place, it would not be considered littering. When large crowds leave a ballpark, movie, theater, concert, or circus, what remains among the seats and aisles is not and *cannot* be litter. It is garbage, dirt, or waste, but not litter. After normal working hours in the downtown area of our cities, a horde of cleaners descend upon the privately owned banks, stores, restaurants, office buildings, factories, etc.

What they do is *clean*, and under no circumstances do they pick up litter. Concurrent with this, the department of sanitation cleans the public streets and sidewalks, picking up *litter*.

Now there is no real distinction to be drawn between leaving garbage in public places and leaving garbage in private places. There is no reason to call the former and not the latter "littering," since what is being done in both cases is the same. In both cases, the creation of garbage is a concomitant of the process of producing or of consuming.

In some instances, leaving garbage to be picked up later is the optimal solution. For example, it is too time-consuming for a carpenter to clean up the wood shavings as he works. It is easier and cheaper to allow the "litter" (wood shavings) to accumulate and be swept away at the end of the day or at periodic intervals. The factory manager *could* institute an anti-"litter" campaign and force the carpenters to keep their work area free of any accumulation of wood shavings. He might even enforce this edict with the threat of a $50 fine. However, with these rules his workforce might quit, or, if they did not quit, the costs of production would rise inordinately, and he would lose business to competitive factories.

In the medical practice, on the other hand, littering cannot be tolerated. Operating, consulting, or treatment rooms must be sanitary, well-scrubbed and free of debris. Failure to adopt a strong anti-litter campaign here would involve the administrator of the hospital in financial failure, as it became known that his institution was unsanitary.

In the case of consumption, most restaurants, for example, do not pursue anti-litter campaigns. There are no signs on restaurant walls forbidding the dropping of forks, napkins, or bread crumbs. A restaurant *could* prohibit litter, but it would lose its customers to other establishments.

What these seemingly disparate examples have in common is to illustrate that in the *market*, the decision of whether and how much litter to allow is based ultimately on the wishes and desires of the consumers! The question is not treated simplistically and there is no general outcry to "get rid of litterbugs."

"Hey, Bozo, you want a citation for litterin'? Pick up that matchbook cover!"

There is rather, a careful weighing of the costs and benefits of allowing waste materials to accumulate. To the extent that the costs of garbage collection are low and the harm caused by garbage accumulating is high, there tend to be frequent collections and severe penalties for leaving garbage around, as in the example given of littering in a medical facility. If the costs of garbage collection are high and the harm caused by the accumulation is low, there tend to be less frequent collections and no penalties for littering. These differences in policy are not the result of any governmental law, but are a result of the market process. Entrepreneurs who do not act in accordance with an accurate cost-benefit analysis lose customers, either directly, as customers stalk out in anger, or indirectly, as the higher costs of operation allow the competition price advantages.

A system which is based on the needs and desires of the people involved is very flexible. In each example, a policy on littering was tailored to the requirements of the specific situation. Moreover, such a system is capable of responding quickly to changes, whether they be in the costs of litter collection or in the harm caused by uncollected litter. If, for instance, a system were installed in hospitals enabling litter to be taken out at very little cost, or if consumer desires regarding litter underwent a marked change, hospital administrators would have to relax their stringent anti-litter stance. The hospitals which failed to adjust to the new technology and tastes would tend to lose patients to competing institutions. (These are private, profit making hospitals. Public hospitals, which obtain their funds through compulsory taxation, have no such incentives to please customers.)

On the other hand, if it were discovered that soda cans and popcorn boxes, left under the seats at baseball stadiums, were disease carriers, or interfered with the viewing of the game, the stadium rules concerning litter would be changed *automatically* by stadium owners, without any government edict.

In considering litter in the public domain, there is no finely attuned system responding to the needs and desires of the people. Rather, the public domain is the ward of the government, and the government treats consumer demands in a rather cavalier manner, virtually ignoring them. Government enterprise is the only enterprise that will deal with an increased desire to litter with a steadfast determination to eliminate it, thereby refusing to adapt to either consumer desires or changing technology.[1] The law is

---

[1]Only a nonprofit government agency could react to increased consumer desires for road use (traffic tie-ups) with a threat to ban cars. Only

the law. The government can function this way because it is outside the market. It does not obtain its revenues from the market process of voluntary trade. It obtains its revenues through taxation, a process completely unrelated to its ability to satisfy customers.

The governmental argument against litter is that it is done out of disrespect for others' rights. But this argument is without merit. The whole concept of private litter is a case in point. If litter were a violation of rights and a refusal to consider the comfort of others, what of the "litter" in restaurants, ballparks, factories, etc.? Litter comes about in the private market precisely as a means of *satisfying* the desires of consumers for comfort. One no more violates the restaurant owner's rights by littering than by eating, since both are *paid* for.

How is the government's failure to maintain a flexible litterbug policy in the public sector to be interpreted? It is not entirely due to indifference, although it is far simpler to totally prohibit something than to deal with it in a reasonable manner. The explanation is that no government, no matter how interested or beneficent, could maintain a flexible litterbug policy. Such a policy must be supported by a price system—a profit and loss system—to measure the cost and benefits of littering, and to automatically penalize managers who failed to adjust accordingly. If the government enacted a system of this type, it would no longer be a governmental system, for it could not rely on the *bête noir* of government—a tax system completely unrelated to success in satisfying the wants of consumers.

The inability of the government to be flexible can occasionally take strange turns. For many years there was no effective restriction in New York City of dog owners who allowed their dogs to defecate on the streets and sidewalks. Presently there is a movement afoot to prohibit dog defecation on any street or

---

a government agency free from the necessity of earning profits could react to increased consumer desires for park use by forbidding people to enter parks after dark.

sidewalk, launched by citizens' groups organized under the banner of "children before dogs." The flexibility of the market is completely ignored by both of these factions. Nowhere is it realized that dog "litter" can be *restricted to certain places*. The issue is seen as a choice between prohibiting it altogether or allowing it everywhere. Imagine the beneficent results that would ensue if the streets and sidewalks were privately owned. A greater flexibility would result because of the rewards entrepreneurs would gain for devising methods of satisfying *both* groups.

Some might object to the private ownership of the sidewalks on the grounds that dog owners would have to pay for the use of a "dog lot" which they now use free (assuming, there is no prohibition of dog defecation). But this is incorrect, because no individual, including the dog owner, has the free use of the sidewalks. The sidewalks, as all other goods and services provided by the government, are paid for by the citizens through taxes! Citizens pay not only for the original cost of the sidewalks, but also for upkeep, maintenance, policing, and cleaning services.

It is difficult to anticipate the exact way a free market would function in this area, but some guesses may be hazarded. Perhaps several enterprising entrepreneurs could set up fenced-in sandy areas which dogs could use. These entrepreneurs could have two separate contracts, one, with the dog owners, which would specify the fee for use of the area, the other with garbage truck owners, specifying the cost of maintaining the areas. The exact location and number of these areas would, as with any service, be determined by the needs of the people involved.

In the light of the inflexibility of the government, and its apparent lack of interest in accommodating public tastes, how is the litterbug to be viewed? The litterbug treats public property in much the same way he would treat private property if he were but free to. Namely, he leaves garbage around on it. It has been demonstrated that there is nothing intrinsically evil about this activity, and that but for governmental calcification, it would be as widely accepted in the public arena as it is in the private. It is an activity which should be regulated by people's needs, not by government fiat.

We must conclude, therefore, that far from being a public enemy, the litterer is actually a hero. The courage exhibited by the litterer, given the intense campaign of vilification directed against him, is considerable. Even more important, the behavior of the litterer who purposefully "takes the law into his own hands" can serve as a protest against an unjust system.

28

THE WASTEMAKERS

People have long suspected that a basic business practice is to purposely manufacture products which are inferior. Businessmen, it is assumed, do not want to turn out high-quality, long lasting products. Instead, they manufacture shoddy products with "built-in" or "planned" obsolescence. When these products wear out, they must be replaced, thus manufacturers stay in business and prosper. This idea, always with us even if somewhat below the surface, received an unneeded, but widely publicized shot in the arm several years ago with the publication of Vance Packard's book, *Waste Makers*.[1]

The theory of "built-in" obsolescence is fallacious. And, with the advent of the ecology movement and the neo-Malthusian Zero Population Growth adherents, it is more important than ever to lay the fallacy to rest. According to the overpopulationists, we have or are soon going to have too many people *in relation to the earth's resources*. In the view of the environmentalists, we are (that is, the free-market system is) presently wasting the resources we have. In the view of still others, built-in obsolescence is a tragic, totally unnecessary component of this waste.

---

[1] Vance Packard, *Waste Makers* (New York: David McKay, 1960).

213

Taken together, these groups pose an intellectual, moral, and even physical threat to a healthy and sane economy.

It is important to begin this critique by noting a truism. Either it costs more to build a product in the "proper" way, so that it does not wear out "before its time," or it does not. A product is shoddy because the manufacturer instructs the workers to turn out inferior merchandise, or because it is cheaper to make it that way.

A true example of built-in obsolescence is the case where no cost saving is gained by making an inferior product. It is as if a time bomb were placed in an otherwise sound piece of merchandise. The consumer does not know it, but the object is scheduled to "self-destruct." This practice clearly *is* wasteful. In economic parlance, society is forgoing higher quality goods which have no alternative uses.

Such behavior, however, will not take place in a private enterprise market economy because it is not survival oriented. Businessmen who engage in planned obsolescence of this sort will decrease their profits, increase their losses, and eventually go bankrupt. Some customers will surely stop buying from a firm which sells inferior quality merchandise at standard prices, and patronize other firms which sell standard quality merchandise at the same standard prices. The firm in question will lose customers, without any compensation in the form of lower costs, and the other firms will gain the customers lost by the wastemaking company.

But the fear which many consumers have is not that *one* businessman will manufacture products with built-in obsolescence, but that all manufacturers will. In that case, it is supposed, the consumer would be trapped.

What would the consequences be if all the manufacturers in an industry agreed, via a cartel arrangement, to turn out low-quality products in order to increase replacement sales? It seems clear that every manufacturer who was a party to the agreement would be powerfully tempted to raise the quality of the goods he was making—in other words, to cheat on the agreement. Because if all the others were turning out products of the same poor quality (as they agreed to do) and he made products which were only slightly better, he would gain customers and increase his profits. Given the profit motive (which was the incentive for the cartel) the members are not likely to honor the agreement.

Second, there will be great temptations for businessmen outside the cartel agreement to enter the industry. By turning out products even slightly better than those turned out by the cartel manufacturers, they will attract customers and profits.

Paradoxically, the forces tending to break up the cartel would become stronger as the cartel became more successful. For the stronger the cartel, the greater the decrease in the quality of the product. The lower the quality, the easier it would become to attract competitors' customers. Even a slight increase in quality would accomplish this.

Advertising also hastens the process of breaking up cartels which try to restrict quality. In fact, advertising tends to prevent their formation in the first place. Advertising builds up brand names with attached good will. The brand name stands for a certain level of quality. If a firm allows the quality of its product to deteriorate, it loses the good will it has spent millions attaining.

Independent rating agencies like Consumers Union also tend to prevent cartels from forming, and to break them up if they do occur. By keeping strict tabs on the quality of merchandise, such rating agencies keep the public apprised of even slight deteriorations of quality.

Finally, even if all members maintain the agreement, and no outsiders step in, the restriction on quality is still more likely to fail than to succeed. For it is impossible for all manufacturers to restrict quality to exactly the same degree. The ones who restrict quality least will inevitably gain better reputations, more customers, and increased profits. The market will continue to be a testing ground, weeding out companies which produce inferior goods. Failing the test means bankruptcy; passing the test means survival.

It seems clear then, that in a free market, cartels cannot be maintained. But they can be maintained, and built-in obsolescence with them, if the government steps in. For example, when the government sets up guild-like restrictions on entry into an industry, cartels are encouraged because competition is discouraged. Thus the interests of those already in the field are protected. Whatever agreements they may have made with one another can be maintained. If they have agreed, as a matter of policy, to restrict the quality of production, that policy has a chance to succeed. The effects of government participation can be seen in many fields. Consider medicine. The government, at the behest of the American Medical Association, has succeeded in banning the use of acupuncture. Acupuncture practitioners threatened the positions of licensed doctors, and the AMA, which functions as a cartel, exerted great pressure against them. This was, of course, in line with its general policy of keeping doctors' salaries high regardless of the quality of service. In the same way, psychologists and psychiatrists, with the help of the government, harass practitioners who are in competition with them. They are seeking to ban all those (encounter group leaders, etc.), whom they themselves have not licensed to practice.

The government has also at times prevented the operation of the internal forces which tend to break up cartels. The railroad cartel is a case in point. Member companies of the railroad cartel agreed to cut back on the quantity of service in order to force prices up. But, as could have been predicted, with higher prices there were fewer passengers. Each railroad began to try to attract the customers of the other railroads by cutting back on the stated price. This would of course have destroyed the cartel. As it happened, the price-cutting took the form of price rebates. But instead of allowing this practice to continue, and thus ruin the waste-making cartel, the government prohibited railroad rebates. And the railroad industry has not recovered yet.

A third way in which the government contributes to the problem of built-in obsolescence is by propping up companies which, because of the low quality of the goods they produce, cannot survive the competition of the market. Many of the subsidies that the government makes available to businessmen serve only to support businesses which are failing because they have been unable to serve their customers.

Let us now consider the second alternative, the case where it costs more money to increase the quality of the product. Here the analysis is just the opposite. This kind of planned obsolescence occurs on the unhampered market every day, but it is by no means wasteful or senseless! It is part and parcel of the choice of quality offered to consumers.

Consider the following hypothetical table of the cost of automobile tires and the life expectancy of each tire.

Brand	Cost	Average Longevity
Tire A	$10	1 year
Tire B	$50	2 years
Tire C	$150	5 years

When purchasing tires, the consumer is given a choice between higher quality, and higher-priced tires, or lower quality, and lower priced tires. Of course the $10 tire is not expected to last as long as the $150 tire! It was made in such a way that it will wear out sooner. This might be termed "built-in" obsolescence. But where is the waste? There is none. The manufacturers of cheap tires are not taking advantage of a helpless consumer market. They are not trapping people into buying low quality goods. They are manufacturing what people want. If some manufacturers of low quality tires were convinced by the ecologists that their products were "wasteful," and stopped producing them, the price of the low quality tires still available would simply rise, because the demand would continue to exist while the supply decreased. This would in turn set up irresistible pressures for manufacturers to get back into (or enter for the first time) the low quality tire field, as profits there began to rise. In this way the market would tend to bring about consumer satisfaction.

The lowly paper plate can serve to further illustrate the point that built-in obsolescence is not wasteful when low quality products are cheaper to make than high quality products. Who would ever think of blaming paper plate manufacturers for built-in obsolescence? Yet there is the same quality-price combination of choices in plates as in the tires. One can buy, at increasing prices, paper plates, plastic plates of varying quality, ceramic and clay baked plates, on and up through plates of the finest quality china.

It is indeed strange that people blame built-in obsolescence for breakdowns in their cars, and *not* for the rapid deterioration of their paper napkins. But in *both* cases there is higher quality merchandise available, at higher prices. The choice is the consumer's. There is no more sense in complaining that low quality cars break down than there is in complaining that paper cups do not last very long. Less expensive products are not made to last as long as more expensive products! That is why they cost less. Clearly, built-in obsolescence which reflects consumer choice is not wasteful.

But isn't low quality in and of itself wasteful because it uses up our resources? Even if built-in obsolescence is not a problem in paper plates, aren't paper plates themselves wasteful because they use up wood?

One problem with this way of looking at the matter is that it assumes that lower quality products use up more resources than higher quality products. To be sure, the lower the quality of the product, the more likely it is that replacement and repair will be necessary. But, on the other hand, higher quality products use up more resources at the outset! The issue is really one between a high initial outlay and small subsequent outlays for a high quality product, versus a low initial outlay and greater subsequent outlays (repairs, replacements) for low quality products.

In a free market, the *consumers* decide between these alternatives. Products are made which are least wasteful *in the view of the consumers*. If consumers decide that, given rapid changes in fashion, it is wasteful to buy clothing that lasts for five years or more, manufacturers will find it more profitable to produce less durable, less expensive clothing. If the market called for it, manufacturers would offer clothing made out of paper. Similarly, if consumers wanted cars that would last longer, producers would offer such cars. They would offer them at a higher price, if consumers wanted these with all the present frills and comforts. If the consumers preferred, the manufacturers would offer them at the same price as lower quality cars, but without the extras.

Furthermore, in a free market, "using up" resources does not pose a serious threat. As scarcities develop, powerful forces automatically come into play to correct them. For example, if wood were to fall into short supply, its price would be forced up. As a consequence, consumers would buy fewer products made of wood. Producers would tend to substitute other materials for wood wherever possible. Cabinets, furniture, boats, etc., would be made of other, less expensive materials. New, possibly synthetic, materials would be developed. Greater care would be taken to recycle the suddenly more valuable "used" wood. Old newsprint, for example, would be chemically treated and reused with greater efforts. The increased price of wood would provide incentives for entrepreneurs to plant more seedlings and take care of forests more intensively. In short, given a dearth of one or even several resources, a free economy automatically adjusts. As long as its adjustment mechanism, the price system, is not interfered with, other cheaper and more plentiful resources will be substituted, and those in short supply will be better preserved.

But what would happen, it may be asked, if not just one or several, but *all* resources were in short supply? What would happen if we depleted all our resources at the same time? This is the stuff from which science fiction is made, so we will have to indulge in a bit of science fiction ourselves to deal with it. But we will stop short of assuming that everything magically vanishes from the face of the earth. In that eventuality, we would have nothing helpful to suggest.

In order to make sense of the view, we will not assume that all resources suddenly disappear, or that the earth suddenly shrinks and shrivels away, but that economic resources get used up and turn into ashes, waste, and dust. For example, we will assume not that coal disappears entirely, but that it gets used up and replaced by ashes, dust, pollutants, and chemical derivatives of the burning process. We will also assume that all other resources get "used up" in the same sense; that is, that they become useless to us.

To deal with this horror, two things must be borne in mind. First, there is good reason to believe that new sources of energy will be discovered or invented as present sources are depleted. There are no reasons to assume that this will not be the case. The human race has passed from the stone age, to the bronze age, to the iron age. When coal sources were depleted, oil was used. After oil, there will be other sources of energy, possibly nuclear. To ignore this technological phenomenon would be to hopelessly distort the issue.

In the second place, we must realize that the direct and indirect source of all energy is the sun. It is the source of every type of energy presently used, and it will be the source of whatever types of energy our technology may produce in the future. But the sun itself will not last forever. When it goes, humanity goes, unless we are technologically advanced enough to either re-energize the sun or relocate on another planet with a younger sun. Whether we will have a technology competent to accomplish this when the time comes depends on choices we are making now. If we exploit the resources of the earth, use them, find replacements for them, and learn from such exploitation, our technology will continue to develop. If we do not, and are motivated by fear, and have no faith in our ability to meet challenges, we will hoard the resources we have at present, and we will not grow any further. We will be waiting, ostrich-like, for the sun to go out and the world to end, having forgone the advanced technology that only increased population and exploitation of the resources the earth makes possible.

VIII. Labor

29

THE FAT CAPITALIST-PIG EMPLOYER

"If not for the minimum wage law and other progressive legislation, the employers, the fat-capitalist-pig exploiting employers, to be precise, would lower wages to whatever level they wanted. At best, we would be pushed back to the days of the sweatshop; at worst, to the days of the industrial revolution and before, when mankind waged an often losing battle with starvation."

So goes the conventional wisdom on the merits of minimum wage legislation. It will be shown, however, that this conventional wisdom is wrong, tragically wrong. It assumes a villain where none exists. What does the law actually accomplish and what are its consequences?

The minimum wage law is, on the face of it, not an employment law but an unemployment law. It does not force an employer to *hire* an employee at the minimum wage level, or at any other level. It compels the employer *not* to hire the employee at certain wage levels, namely, those below the minimum set by law. It coerces the *worker*, no matter how anxious he may be to accept a job at a wage level below the minimum, *not* to accept the job. It obligates the worker who is faced with a choice between a low-wage job and unemployment to choose unemployment. Nor does the law even push any wage up; it only lops *off* jobs which do not meet the standard.

How would wages be determined in the absence of minimum wage legislation? If the labor market consists of many suppliers of labor (employees) and many demanders of labor (employers), then the wage rate will tend to be set in accordance with what the economist calls the "marginal productivity of labor." The marginal productivity of labor is the extra amount of receipts an employer would have if he employs a given worker. In other words, if by adding a given worker to the payroll, the employer's total receipts rise by $60 per week, then the marginal productivity of that worker is $60 per week. The wage rate paid to the worker tends to equal the worker's marginal productivity. Why is this so, in view of the fact that the employer would prefer to pay the worker virtually nothing, no matter what his productivity? The answer is, competition between employers.

For example, assume the worker's marginal productivity is equal to $1.00 per hour. If he were hired at 5¢ per hour, the employer would make 95¢ per hour profit. Other employers would bid for that worker. Even if they paid him 6¢, 7¢, or 10¢ an hour, their profit would still make the bidding worthwhile. The bidding would end at the wage level of $1.00 per hour. For only when the wages paid equal the worker's marginal productivity will the incentive to bid for the worker stop.

But suppose the employers mutually *agree* not to hire workers at more than 5¢ per hour? This occurred in the Middle Ages when cartels of employers got together, *with the aid of the state*, to pass laws which prohibited wage levels above a certain maximum. Such agreements can only succeed with state aid and there are good reasons why this is so.

In the noncartel situation, the employer hires a certain number of workers—the number which he believes will yield the maximum profit. If an employer hires only ten workers, it is because he thinks the productivity of the tenth will be greater than the wage he must pay and that the productivity of an eleventh would be less than this amount.

If, then, a cartel succeeds in lowering the wage of workers with a marginal productivity of $1.00 to 5¢ per hour, each employer will want to hire many more workers. This is known as the "law of downward sloping demand" (the lower the price, the more buyers will want to purchase). The worker whose productivity was, in the eyes of the employer, just below $1.00, and therefore not worth hiring at $1.00 per hour, will be eagerly sought at 5¢ per hour.

This leads to the first flaw in the cartel: each employer who is a party to the cartel has a great financial incentive to cheat. Each employer will try to bid workers away from the others. The only way he can do this is by offering higher wages. How much higher? All the way up to $1.00, as we have seen before, and for the same reason.

The second flaw is that nonmembers of the cartel arrangement would want to hire these workers at 5¢ per hour, even assuming no "cheating" by members. This also tends to drive up the wage from 5¢ to $1.00 per hour. Others, such as would-be employers in noncartel geographical areas, self-employed artisans who could not before afford employees, and employers who had previously hired only part-time workers, would all contribute to an upward trend in the wage level.

Even if the workers themselves are ignorant of wage levels paid elsewhere, or are located in isolated areas where there is no alternative employment, these forces will apply. It is not necessary that *both parties* to a trade have knowledge of all relevant conditions. It has been said that unless both parties are equally well-informed, "imperfect competition" results, and economic laws somehow do not apply. But this is mistaken. Workers usually have little overall knowledge of the labor market, but employers are supposedly much better informed. And this is all that is necessary. While the worker may not be well-informed about alternative job opportunities, he knows well enough to take the highest paying job. All that is necessary is that the employer present himself to the employee who is earning less than his marginal productivity, and offer him a higher wage.

"You must stop this insane diet, J.T.—so what if the union does call you a 'FAT CAPITLISTIC PIG'!"

And this is exactly what naturally happens. The self-interest of employers leads them "as if by an invisible hand" to ferret out low-wage workers, offer them higher wages, and spirit them away. The whole process tends to raise wages to the level of marginal productivity. This applies not only to urban workers, but to workers in isolated areas who are ignorant of alternative job opportunities and would not have the money to get there even if aware of them. It is true that the differential between the wage level and the productivity of the unsophisticated worker will have to be great enough to compensate the employer for the costs of coming to the worker, informing him of job alternatives, and paying the costs of sending him there. But this is almost always the case, and employers have long been cognizant of it.

The Mexican "wetbacks" are a case in point. Few groups have less knowledge of the labor market in the United States, and less money for traveling to more lucrative jobs. Not only do employers from southern California travel hundreds of miles to find them, but they also furnish trucks or travel money to transport them northward. In fact, employers from as far away as Wisconsin travel to Mexico for "cheap labor" (workers receiving less than their marginal product). This is eloquent testimony to the workings of an obscure economic law they have never heard of. (There are complaints about the poor working conditions of these migrant workers. But these complaints are mainly from either well-intentioned people who are unaware of the economic realities, or from those not in sympathy with these hapless workers receiving full value for their labors. The Mexican workers *themselves* view the package of wages and working conditions as favorable compared to alternatives at home. This is seen in their willingness, year after year, to come to the United States during the harvesting season.)

It is not the minimum wage law, therefore, that stands between Western civilization and a return to the stone age. There are market forces and profit maximizing behavior on the part of entrepreneurs, which ensure that wages do not fall below the level of productivity. And the level of productivity is itself determined by technology, education, and the amount of capital equipment in a society, not by the amount of "socially progressive" legislation enacted. Minimum wage legislation does not do what its press claims. What *does* it do? What are its actual effects?

What will be the reaction of the typical worker to a legislated increase in wages from $1.00 to $2.00? If he is already fully employed, he may want to work more hours. If he is partially employed or unemployed, it is virtually certain that he will want to work more.

The typical employer, on the other hand, will react in the opposite way. He will want to fire virtually all of the workers he is forced to give raises to. (Otherwise he would have granted raises before he was compelled to.) Now, he has to keep production up, so he might not be able to adjust this situation immediately. But as time passes he will replace his unexpectedly expensive unskilled workers with fewer but more skilled workers and with more sophisticated machinery, so that his total productivity remains constant.

Students of an introductory economics course learn that when a price level above equilibrium is set, the result is a surplus. In the example, when a minimum wage level above $1.00 per hour is set, the result is a surplus of labor—otherwise called unemployment. Iconoclastic as it may sound, it is, therefore, *true* that the minimum wage law causes unemployment. At the higher wage level it creates more people willing to work and fewer jobs available.

The only debatable question is: how much unemployment does the minimum wage law create? This depends on how quickly the unskilled workers are replaced by equivalently productive skilled workers in conjunction with machines. In our own recent history, for example, when the minimum wage law increased from 40¢ to 75¢ per hour, elevator operators began to be replaced. It has taken some time, but most elevators are now automatic. The same thing happened to unskilled dishwashers. They have been and are still being replaced by automatic dishwashing machinery, operated and repaired by semi-skilled and skilled workers. The process continues. As the minimum wage law is applied to greater and greater segments of the unskilled population, and as its level rises, more and more unskilled people will become unemployed.

Finally, it is important to note that a minimum wage law only directly affects those earning less than the minimum wage level. A law requiring that everyone be paid at least $2.00 per hour has no effect on an individual earning $10.00 per hour. But before assuming that the minimum wage law simply results in pay raises for low-wage earners, consider what would happen if a $100.00 per hour minimum wage law went into effect. How many of us have such great productivity that an employer would be willing to pay $100.00 for an hour of our services? Only those thought to be worth that much money would retain their jobs. The rest would be unemployed. The example is extreme, of course, but the principle which *would* operate if such a law were passed *does* operate now. When wages are raised by law, the workers with low productivity are discharged.

Who is hurt by the minimum wage law? The unskilled, whose productivity level is below the wage level legislated. The unemployment rate of black male teenagers is usually (under-) estimated at 50 percent, three times the unemployment level of the 1933 depression. And this percentage does not even begin to take into account the great numbers who have given up searching for a job in the face of this unemployment rate.

The lost income that this represents is only the tip of the iceberg. More important is the on-the-job-training these young men could be receiving. Were they *working* at $1.00 per hour (or even less) instead of being *unemployed* at $2.00 per hour, they would be learning skills that would enable them to raise their productivity and wage rates above $2.00 in the future. Instead they are condemned to street corners, idleness, learning only those skills which will earn them jail sentences at some early future time.

One of the greatest hurdles facing a black teenager is looking for his first job. Every employer demands work experience, but how can the young black get it if no one will hire him? This is not because of some "employer conspiracy" to denigrate minority teenagers. It is because of the minimum wage law. If an employer is *forced* to pay for an experienced-level worker, is it any wonder that he demands this kind of labor?

A paradox is that many black teenagers are worth more than the minimum wage but are unemployed because of it. In order to be employed with a $2.00 an hour minimum wage law, it is not enough just to *be* worth $2.00. You have to be *thought* to be worth $2.00 per hour by an employer who stands to lose money if he guesses wrong and may go broke if he guesses wrong too often.

With a minimum wage law, an employer cannot afford to take a chance. And, unfortunately, black teenagers are frequently viewed as "risky," as a class. When confronted with a reluctant employer, a Horatio Alger hero could stride over manfully and offer to work for a token salary, or even for nothing, for a term of two weeks. During this time our hero would prove to the employer that his productivity deserved a higher wage rate. More important, he would bear with the employer part of the risk of hiring an untried worker. The employer would go along with this arrangement because he would be risking little.

But the Horatio Alger hero did not have to do battle with a minimum wage law which made such an arrangement illegal. The law thus insures that there is less chance for the black teenager to prove his worth in an honest way.

The minimum wage law hurts not only the black teenager, but the black ghetto merchant and industrialist as well. Without this law, he would have access, in a way which his white counterpart would not, to a cheap labor pool of black teenager labor. The young black worker would be more accessible to him since he tends to live in the ghetto and would have easier access to the job site. He would undoubtedly have less resentment toward, and a smoother work relationship with, a black entrepreneur. Since this is one of the most important determinants of productivity for jobs of this type, the black employer could pay his workers more than the white one could—and still make a profit.

Unfortunate as the effects on young black workers are, a greater tragedy of the minimum wage law concerns the handicapped worker (the lame, the blind, the deaf, the amputee, the paralyzed, and the mentally handicapped). The minimum wage law effectively makes it illegal for a profit-seeking employer to hire a handicapped person. All hopes of even a modicum of self-reliance are dashed. The choice the handicapped person faces is between idleness and governmentally supported make-work schemes which consist of trivial activities and are as demoralizing as idleness. That such schemes are supported by a government which makes honest employment impossible in the first place, is an irony few handicapped people would find amusing.

Recently, certain classes of handicapped people (the slightly handicapped) have become exempt from the minimum wage law. It is, therefore, in the interest of employers to hire the "slightly handicapped," and they now have jobs. But if it has been realized that the minimum wage law hurts the employment chances of "slightly handicaped" people, surely it should be realized that it hurts the chances of others. Why are seriously handicapped people not exempt?

If the minimum wage law does not protect the individual it seems designed to protect, whose interests does it serve? Why was such legislation passed?

Among the most vociferous proponents of minimum wage legislation is organized labor—and this must give us pause for thought. For the average union member earns much more than the minimum wage level of $2.00 per hour. If he is already earning $10.00 per hour, as we have seen, his wage level is in accordance with the law, and is not, therefore, affected by it. What then accounts for his passionate commitment to it?

His concern is hardly with the downtrodden worker—his black, Puerto Rican, Mexican-American and American-Indian brethren. For his union is typically 99.44 percent white, and he strenuously resists the attempts by members of minority groups to enter his union. What then stands behind organized labor's interest in minimum wage legislation?

When the minimum wage law forced up the wages of unskilled labor, the law of downward sloping demand caused employers to substitute skilled labor for unskilled labor. In the same way, when a labor union, composed mainly of skilled laborers, obtains a wage increase, the law of downward sloping demand causes employers to substitute unskilled laborers for skilled laborers! In other words, because skilled and unskilled laborers are, within certain bounds, substitutable for each other, they are actually in competition with one another. It might well be that it is 10 or 20 unskilled workers who are in competition with, and hence substitutable for two or three skilled workers, plus a more sophisticated machine. But of the substitutability itself, especially in the long run, there can be no doubt.

What better way to get rid of your competition than to force it to price itself out of the market? What better way for a union to insure that the next wage hike will not tempt employers to hire unskilled, nonunion scabs (especially minority group members)? The tactic is to get a law passed that makes the wage of the unskilled so high that they cannot be hired, no matter how outrageous the wage demands of the union are. (If minority groups could get a law passed requiring all *union* wages to rise ten times their present amount, they could virtually destroy the unions. Union membership would decline precipitously. Employers would fire all unionists, and in cases where they could not, or did not, they would go bankrupt.)

Do the unions purposefully and knowingly advocate such a harmful law? It is not motives that concern us here. It is only acts and their effects. The effects of the minimum wage law are disastrous. It adversely affects the poor, the unskilled, and minority group members, the very people it was supposedly designed to help.

30

THE SCAB

One of the most universally shared attitudes is that the scab is a wretched character. He is unscrupulous and sneakily in league with the "boss." Together, scab and boss plot to deprive union workers of their rights, and of the jobs that are legitimately theirs. Scabs are hired to force union workers to accept lower wages. When it becomes known that scabs are also used to beat up union workers and pickets, the case is virtually complete—the scab is the greatest enemy of the worker.

These are the facts that are taught in many of our centers of learning, to be challenged only at the risk of one's reputation as a scholar. Nevertheless, this flummery must be refuted.

The first point to establish is that a job is not a thing which can be owned by a worker—or by anyone else. A job is the manifestation of a *trade* between a worker and an employer. The worker trades his labor for the money of the employer, at some mutually agreeable rate of exchange. So when we speak of "my job," we are only talking figuratively.

Although we are in the habit of using such phrases as "my job," "my customer," and "my tailor," we do not presume ownership in *any* of these instances. Take first the case of "my customer." If this phrase were taken literally, it would denote that the merchant has an ownership right over the "custom" of the people who habitually buy from him. He would *own* the customer's patronage and he would, therefore, have a right to object if "his" customer patronized another merchant.

The sword cuts both ways. Let us take the case of "my tailor." If we were to take this phrase literally, we would have to say that the tailor may not shut down his shop, relocate, or declare himself bankrupt, without the permission of the customers. He is "their" tailor.

In both these cases, of course, it is clear that the possessive pronoun is not meant to imply literal possession. Clearly, neither buyer or seller has the right to insist upon the permanence of a business relationship, unless of course, a long-term contract has been agreed upon by both parties. Then, and only then, would the merchant and the customer have the right to object if either party ended the relationship without the consent of the other.

Now let us consider "my job." What is the worker implying when he objects to the scab taking "his" job away? The worker is arguing as though he *owned* the job. He is, in other words, assuming that service, after a certain period of time, obligates the employer to the employee as strictly as if they had agreed to a contract. But in fact, the employer has never obligated himself contractually.

One wonders how the workers would react if the principle upon which their anti-scab feeling is based were adopted by the employer. How would they feel if employers assumed the right to *forbid* long-term workers from leaving their employment? What if he accused another employer who dared to hire "his" worker of being a scab! Yet the situation is entirely symmetrical.

Clearly, there is something wrong with an argument which asserts that once people *voluntarily* agree to trade, they are thereafter *compelled* to *continue* to trade. By what shift in logic is a voluntary relationship converted into a strictly involuntary relationship? Hiring an individual does not imply slave-holding rights over that person, nor does having worked for an employer give one the *right to a job*. It should be evident that the worker never "owns" the job, that it is not "his" job. The scab, therefore,

is guilty of no irregularity when he takes the job which the worker formerly held.

The issue of violence between workers and scabs is a separate issue. The initiation of violence is condemnable, and when scabs initiate violence, they deserve our censure. But the initiation of violence is not their defining characteristic. When they engage in it, they do so as individuals, not as scabs *qua* scabs. Milkmen, after all, sometimes go berserk and commit aggression against nonaggressors. No one would take this as proof that the delivery of milk is an intrinsically evil enterprise. In like manner, the use of illegitimate violence on the part of scabs does not render the enterprise of scabbing illegitimate.

In recent times, the muddled and inconsistent thinking about scabs has become increasingly evident. Liberals, traditionally most vociferous in denouncing scabs, have of late shown signs of confusion on this issue. They have come to realize that in virtually all cases the scabs are poorer than the workers they seek to replace. And liberals have almost always championed the poor worker. Also, the specter of racism has been raised. In many cases, black scabs have been pitted against white (unionized) workers, Mexican workers against Mexican-American workers, Japanese workers against higher paid American workers.

The Ocean Hill-Brownsville decentralization school board clash in Brooklyn, New York, is a dramatic case in point. Under the local school board system, Rhody McCoy, the black school board administrator, fired several white teachers for alleged racist behavior toward their young black pupils. In response, the white dominated United Federation of Teachers Union struck the entire New York City educational system, including Ocean Hill-Brownsville. If the black Ocean Hill-Brownsville school district was to continue to function, unit administrator McCoy would have to find replacements for the striking white teachers. He did, and they were, naturally, scabs. Hence, the quandary faced by the liberals: on the one hand, they were unalterably opposed to scabs, but on the other hand, they were unalterably opposed to the racism of the United Federation of Teachers. Clearly, there was more heat than light in their attitudes.

Scabs obviously have been unjustly maligned. Employment does not give the employee any proprietary privileges closed to workers who wish to compete for the same job. Scabbing and free competition are opposite sides of the same coin.

31

THE RATE BUSTER

The scene is familiar from hundreds of movies featuring labor themes: the young eager worker comes to the factory for the first time, determined to be a productive worker. In his enthusiasm, he happily produces more than the other workers who have been at the factory many years, and who are tired, stooped, and arthritic. He is a "rate buster."

Not unnaturally, antipathy springs up between our eager young worker and his senior colleagues. After all, they are cast in a slothful role. In contrast to his youthful exuberance, their production levels look meager indeed.

As the young worker continues his accelerated work output, he becomes more and more alienated from the other workers. He becomes haughty. The older workers, for their part, try to treat him with compassion. But when he remains resistant, they subject him to a silent treatment and commit him to a worker's purgatory.

As the film continues, there occurs a climactic moment when the youthful rate buster comes to his senses. This comes about in any number of ways, all dramatic. Perhaps he sees a sick old woman, an ex-factory worker, or a worker who has been injured in the factory. If the movie in question is *avant garde*, the conversion can be sparked through the good offices of a cat grousing around in an overturned garbage can. Whatever the method, the young man does come to see the error of his ways.

Then, in the last dramatic scene, which usually ends with all the workers—reformed rate buster included—walking off arm-in-arm, a kindly old worker-philosopher takes over center stage. He gives the young worker a five-minute course in labor history, from ancient Roman times down to the present, showing the constant perfidy of the "bosses," and proving beyond question that the only hope of the workers lies in "solidarity."

There has always been, he explains, a class struggle between the workers and the capitalists, with the workers continually struggling for decent wages and working conditions. The bosses are portrayed as always trying to pay the workers less than they deserve, pushing them as far as they can until they drop from exhaustion. Any worker who cooperates with the bosses in their unceasing, merciless, and ruthless efforts to "speed up" the workers, and to force them to increase their productivity levels, is an enemy of the working class. With this summation by the worker-philosopher, the movie ends.

This view of labor economics contains a tangle of fallacies which is interwoven with each part resting in complex ways on other parts. However, there is one core fallacy.

The core fallacy is the assumption that *there is only so much work to be done in the world*. Sometimes called the "lump of labor" fallacy, this economic view holds that the peoples of the world only require a limited amount of labor in their behalf. When this amount is surpassed, there will be no more work to be done, and hence, there will be no more jobs for the workers. For those who hold this view, limiting the productivity of the eager young workers is of overriding importance. For if these workers work too hard, they will ruin things for everyone. By "hogging up" the limited amount of work which exists, they leave too little for everyone else. It is as if the amount of work that can be done resembles a pie of a fixed size. If some people take more than their share, everyone else will suffer with less.

If this economic view of the world were correct, there would indeed be some justification for the theory espoused by the labor-philosopher of the movie. There would be some justification for insisting that the younger and more active worker not take away more than his share of the "pie." However, adherence to this theory has proved to be inefficient and uneconomic, with tragic results.

This false view is based upon the assumption that people's desires—for creature comforts, leisure, intellectual, and aesthetic achievements—have a sharp upward boundary which can be reached in a finite amount of time; and that when it is reached, production must cease. Nothing could be further from the truth.

To assume that human desires can be fully and finally satisfied is to assume that we can reach a point at which human perfection—material, intellectual, and aesthetic—has been fully realized. Paradise? Perhaps. If it were somehow achieved, then certainly there would be no "unemployment" problem—for who would need a job?

There is as much work to be done as there are unfulfilled desires. Since human desires are, for all practical purposes, limitless, the amount of work to be done is also limitless. Therefore, no matter how much work the eager young man completes, he cannot possibly exhaust or even make an appreciable dent in the amount of work to be done.

If the eager worker does not "take work away from others" (because there is a limitless amount of work to be done), what effect *does* he have? The effect of working harder and more efficiently is to increase production. By his energy and efficiency, he increases the size of the pie—the pie that will then be shared among all those who took part in its production.

The rate buster should also be considered from another vantage point. Consider the plight of a family shipwrecked on a tropical island.

When the Swiss Family Robinson sought refuge on an island, their store of belongings consisted only of what was salvaged from the ship. The meager supply of capital goods, plus their own laboring ability, will determine whether or not they survive.

If we strip away all the novelistic superficialities, the economic situation that the Swiss Family Robinson found itself in was facing an unending list of desires, while the means at their disposal for the satisfaction of these desires was extremely limited.

If we suppose that all the members of the family set to work with the material resources at their disposal, we would find that they can satisfy only some of their desires.

What would be the effect of "rate busting" in their situation? Suppose one of the children suddenly becomes a rate buster and is able to produce twice as much per day as the other members of the family. Will this young punk be the ruination of the family, "take work away" from the other family members, and wreak havoc upon the mini-society they have created?

It is obvious that the Swiss Family Robinson rate buster will not bring ruination upon his family. On the contrary, the rate buster will be seen as the hero he is, since there is no danger that his increased productivity would cause the family to run out of work. We have seen that for practical and even philosophical reasons, the wants and desires of the family were limitless. The family would hardly be in trouble even if several members were rate busters.

If the rate busting family member can produce ten extra units of clothing, it may become possible for other members of the family to be relieved of their clothing manufacturing chores. New jobs will be assigned to them. There will be a sorting out period during which it is decided which jobs should be undertaken. But clearly, the end result will be greater satisfaction for the family. In a modern, complex economy, the results would be identical, though the process more complicated. The sorting out period, for example, may take some time. The point remains, however, that because of rate busting, society as a whole will move toward greater and greater satisfaction and prosperity.

Another aspect of rate busting is the creation of *new* items. Thomas Edison, Isaac Newton, Wolfgang Mozart, J.S. Bach, Henry Ford, Jonas Salk, Albert Einstein, plus innumerable others, were the rate busters of their day, not of quantity, but of quality. Each "busted" through what was considered by their society to be a "normal" rate and type of productivity. Yet each of these rate busters contributed incalculably to our civilization.

In addition to understanding rate busting from the point of view of quantity and innovation, rate busting should also be considered in terms of the new lives on this earth that it makes possible. The amount of human life which the earth can support is related to the level of productivity human beings achieve. If there are fewer rate busters, the number of lives this earth can support will be severely limited. If however, the number of rate busters increases significantly in each respective field, the earth will then be able to support an ever-expanding population.

The conclusion then is that not only are rate busters responsible for satisfying more of our desires than a slower, less efficient rate of production, they are also responsible for preserving the very lives of all those who would have to die were it not for the rate busters enlarging the scope of human satisfactions. They provide the means with which the increasing global birth rate can be supported.

32

THE EMPLOYER OF CHILD LABOR

High on the list of the enemies of society, one can always find the employer of child labor—cruel, cold hearted, exploitative, cunning, and evil. In the public mind, child labor is almost equivalent to slave labor, and the children's employer is no better than the slave owner.

It is important to correct this view. Simple justice demands it, for the majority opinion on this question is completely fallacious. The archetypical child labor employer is as kindly, benevolent, and filled with the milk of human kindness as anyone else. Moreover, the institution of child labor is an honorable one, with a long and glorious history of good works. And the villains of the piece are not the employers, but rather those who prohibit the free market in child labor. These do-gooders are responsible for the untold immiseration of those who are thus forced out of employment. Although the harm done was greater in the past, when great poverty made widespread child labor necessary, there are *still* people in dire straits today. Present prohibitions of child labor are thus an unconscionable interference with their lives.

The first plank in the defense is that the employer of child labor has not forced anyone to join his employ. Any and all labor

243

agreements are completely voluntary. As such, unless they were thought to be mutually beneficial, they would not be agreed to.

But in what sense can a labor contract with a child be completely voluntary? Does not complete voluntarism imply an awareness that a child is not capable of? To answer this question, consideration should be given to a proper definition of what a child is.

This is an ancient question which has never been fully resolved. Nevertheless, we shall consider several ages which have been suggested as dividing the child from the adult, analyze them, and then offer an alternative.

Among the earliest ages for the cut-off point between childhood and adulthood are those proposed by the various religions. The age of confirmation into the religion, which usually occurs in the very early teens, or even before, is the age at which many religions define adulthood. But the person (child) at, for example, age 13 also is, except in rare instances, still immature, relatively helpless, and ignorant of the skills necessary to care for himself. So it must be rejected.

The next candidate for adulthood is age 18. Usually picked because this is the age at which a young man becomes eligible for the draft, this age also has several problems as a definition of adulthood. We may start off by questioning whether or not fighting in wars is an "adult" action. All too often, going to war is virtually the opposite of behavior usually indicative of adulthood. Also, merely following orders (the be-all and end-all of the enlisted soldier) cannot be considered an adult paradigm. In addition, there is the problem that the draft, an involuntary institution if ever there was one, serves as the very basis for the order-taking that follows. At least if the original decision to obey orders was made on a voluntary basis, such as the decision to join an orchestra, and then to follow all (musical) orders of the conductor, there might be some adult-like behavior involved in the draft. However, based as it is on original involuntarism, even so much cannot be said for the 18 year old draftable age. Another problem with the 18 year cut-off point is that the original reason for our search was the fear that a mere child would be unable to make *voluntary* contracts on his own. How then can we base such an age on a patently *involuntary* institution such as the draft?

Perhaps the latest candidate for adulthood is the voting age—21 years old. But even this is open to harsh criticism. There is first the problem that several, if not many 10 year olds, have a greater grasp of political, social, historical, psychological, and economic factors, presumably the factors that enable one to vote "wisely," than do many people over the age of 21. One would then think that if this were true, there would be some recognition of the fact in the form of a movement to enfranchise all bright 10 year olds, or rather, all bright children of any age. But this would defeat the original goal of allowing only adults to vote. Through this circularity of reasoning, we can see that the age of 21 is only an arbitrary cutoff point.

We can likewise see all other arbitrary definitions of adulthood to be without merit. What is needed is not an arbitrary age limit which will apply to all people regardless of ability, temperment, and behavior, but rather a criteria which can take all these qualities into account. Moreover, the criteria should be consistent with the libertarian principle of self-ownership of property: namely homesteading. What is wanted is an application of the principle of homesteading, which establishes self-ownership and ownership of property, but applied now to the perplexing problem of when a child becomes an adult.

Such a theory has been put forth by Professor Murray N. Rothbard. According to Rothbard, a child becomes an adult not when he reaches some arbitrary age limit, but rather when he *does* something to establish his ownership and control over his own person: namely, when he leaves home, and becomes able to support himself. This criteria, and only this criteria, is free of all the objections to arbitrary age limits. Moreover, not only is it consistent with the libertarian homesteading theory, it is but an application of it. For by leaving home and becoming his own means of support, the ex-child becomes an *initiator*, as the homesteader, and owes his improved state to his own actions.

"When I was their age my old man got me a job in a boatyard. Man did I have calluses. The kids today got it made."

The theory has several implications. If the only way a child may become an adult is by picking himself up and establishing such adulthood of and by his own volition, then the parent has no right to interfere with this choice. The parent cannot, then, forbid the child from leaving the parental household. The parent has other rights and obligations over the child *as long as the child remains in the house of the parents*. (This accounts for the validity of the oft-heard parental order: "As long as you're in this house, you'll do things my way.") But the one thing the parent cannot do is forbid the child's departure. To do this would be to violate the volitional aspects of growing up from a child to an adult.

It should be noted that this theory of the passage from childhood to adulthood is the only one consistent with the problem of mental deficiency. According to the specific arbitrary theories of adulthood, a mental incompetent, aged 50, ought to be considered an adult, even though he manifestly is not. These theories then come up with further arbitrary *ad hoc* "exceptions" to fit the case. But the mental incompetent is no embarrassment to the homesteading theory. Since he has not (been able to) seized ownership and adulthood of and for himself, the mental incompetent of whatever age is simply not an adult.

The most important implication of the homesteading theory of adulthood is, of course, the one regarding the prohibition of so-called "child" labor, where a child is defined as someone with less than a certain arbitrary number of years. For this prohibition of so-called "child" labor, as in the case of parental interference with the child's decision to leave home, will effectively remove the possibility of "voluntarily" becoming an adult. If a person of tender years is effectively prohibited from working, the option to leave home and to support himself is removed from him. He is then excluded from "homesteading his own adulthood" and must perforce wait until the arbitrary number of years "defining" adulthood has been reached.

However, the adult homesteading theory does not *require* employers to hire young persons who are trying to establish their adulthood. It is, of course, true that unless *some* employer hires such a person, he will find it as difficult to become an adult as in the case where his parents forbade his departure, or the government prohibited it. But the key difference is that the *voluntaristic* nature of the passage from childhood to adulthood will not be infringed upon by employers refusing to hire young people. This is so because true voluntarism requires voluntary action on the part of *both* parties to an agreement. The employer, as well as the employee, must agree. In any case, since there can be no positive obligations, unless the individual himself contracts for them, and the employer has made no advance commitment to employ the youngster, there is no moral obligation on the part of the employer. (Employers will of course, employ young people when they feel it is to their advantage to do so, as they have always done when not prohibited by law.)

Not only is it important to end prohibitions of employment of children for the sake of their peaceful and voluntaristic transition into adulthood; it is also of overriding importance to the small but growing "kid liberation" movement. The prohibition against job opportunities will have to be ended if children are to be truly liberated from their parents while in residence in the parental abode. Of what value is the right to leave the family household and seek a living outside, if a youngster is prohibited from supporting himself? The right of every kid to "fire his parents" if they become too onerous, is completely compromised by the laws against child labor.

Can a labor contract with a mere "child" be truly voluntary, given his tender years, lack of experience, etc.? The answer is yes. A *person*, any person, who has had the ability to leave home and to attempt to earn his own living *is* mature enough to enter into a contract on a voluntary basis, since such a person is a child no longer. The opposite answer, as we have seen, would effectively bar young people from striking out on their own and becoming adults through homesteading. Their only alternative would be to wait until they have reached whatever arbitrary number of years "society," in its infinite wisdom, has determined to be necessary for adulthood.

There are other objections, however, to the legalization of "child" labor. It will be said that a destitute youngster, even though an adult through homesteading, will be taken advantage of by employers; that the employer will "make profit" from the plight the youngster happens to find himself in.

But it would be far *more* harmful if his one source of support, however bleak, were legislated out of existence. Despite the fact that the employer might be cruel, the job menial, and the salary low, it would be far more injurious to forbid him the *opportunity*. If there are other, more favorable, alternatives, the young person will avail himself of them even if the law allows the choice of accepting or rejecting the unfavorable job. If there are no other opportunities, the law prohibiting child labor will take from him this one opportunity, however unfavorable.

In a free market society, the employer will *not* be able to take advantage of the misery of the young worker, if by this it is meant that he will not be able to pay him less than his marginal product. As we have seen in the chapter on the capitalist-pig-employer, there exist powerful forces on an open market which will tend to force all wages up toward the level of productivity of the worker in question.

However destitute and helpless the youngster who is looking for work may be, it is not the fault of the potential employer. Even if the destitution and "lack of bargaining power" of the worker were very extreme, and even if the employer were able to "take advantage of this" (as we have seen is not the case), it would still not be the fault of the employer. If anything, the unfortunate situation would have to be blamed on the background of the (ex-) child.

The question arises as to what degree the parent is obligated to support the child. As a general principle, the parent has no positive obligations whatsoever in regard to the child. The argument to the contrary, that a parent does have some positive obligations toward the child, based upon the supposed contractual nature, or voluntary decision on the part of the parents to bear the child, may be easily shaken. Consider the following:

1. All children are equal in rights due them from their parents, regardless of the way in which they were conceived.

2. Specifically, the child who is a product of rape has as many obligations due him from his female parent as any other child. (We assume that the male parent, the rapist, has gone.) No matter what views we have on rape, the child who is a product of such rape is entirely guiltless of this crime, or any other crime.

3. The voluntary nature of child rearing and conception does not apply in the case of rape.

4. Therefore, the argument that the parent owes some obligations to the child which arise out of the voluntary nature of the conception, or out of an "implicit contract," cannot apply in the case of rape, i.e., in the case of rape, at least, the female parent owes no positive obligation to the child, because she did not consent to its inception.

5. All children, being equally guiltless of any crime, in spite of any theory to the contrary, such as "original sin," have equal rights due them from their parents. Since all such rights (supposedly) flow from the voluntary nature of conception, and the children born of rape manifestly lack this voluntary aspect, they, at least have no rights due them from their (female) parent. *But their rights are equal to those of all other children.* Therefore, no child, whosoever, has any positive obligations due him from his parents.

Nor is it immediately or intuitively obvious that there are any other grounds for establishing any parental duties to children. Given, then, that nothing but a voluntary agreement on the part of the parent *could* establish obligations to children, and that this argument fails, it is obvious that there are no positive obligations incumbent upon parents toward their children.

"No positive obligations" implies that the parent has no more of an obligation to feed, clothe, and shelter his own child than he has to serve the children of other people, or, for that matter, than to serve other adults who are completely unrelated to him, by birth, agreement, etc. This is not to suggest, however, that the parent may kill the child. Just as the parent has no right to kill the children of other parents, he has no right to kill his "own" children, or rather, children he has given birth to.

The parent, when he assumes the role of parenthood, is a sort of caretaker for the child. If ever the parent wishes to relinquish this role that he or she has voluntarily adopted, or not assume this obligation in the first place, she is completely free to do so. She can offer the baby for adoption, or, in the old tradition of the natural law, leave the baby on the steps of a church or charitable institution specializing in the care of children.

But the parent may not secret the baby in a hidden corner of the house without food, or refuse to offer it for adoption, and wait for it to die. To do this would be equivalent to murder—a crime which must always be severely condemned. The parent who keeps the child hidden while starving it (so as not to actually commit violent murder upon it) has renounced his caretakership or the parental relationship others might be willing to assume.

Perhaps the parental-caretaker role may be made clearer by entering it into a hierarchy of homesteading: the child falls into a realm between that of another adult and that of an animal. If one adult helps another, he cannot by that help alone, come to be the owner of the other person. If an adult domesticates an animal, and through his own efforts brings the animal into productive use (productive for mankind), he can thereby come to own it. The child, an intermediate case, can be "owned" through homesteading, but only on a caretaker basis, until he is ready to assert ownership over his own person; namely, to assume adulthood by becoming independent of his parents. The parent can exercise control over the child and rear it only as long as he *continues* his homesteading efforts. (With an animal, or with land, once it is homesteaded, the owner need no longer continue to homestead it in order to own it. He can, for example, be an absentee landlord or animal owner.) If he discontinues his homesteading operations with the child, he must then either offer it for adoption, if it is too young and helpless to fend for itself, or he must allow it to run away to set up its own life, if it is able and willing.

If the parent brought up the child with just enough help and aid to qualify as a continuance of homesteading, but no more, and if the child is in a relatively deprived background, this cannot be laid at the door of the prospective employer. Prohibiting an employer from hiring such a youngster will in no way improve his lot—it can only worsen it.

True, there are parents who make *unwise* decisions concerning children, unwise from the vantage point of outside observers.

It does not follow, however, that the welfare of children will be raised by placing them in the hands of the state apparatus. The state, too, makes unwise, and even *unhealthy* decisions concerning children, and a child can much more easily leave his parent than leave his government, which rules us all.

We must conclude, then, that all labor contracts concerning young people are valid as long as they are voluntary—and they *can* be voluntary. Either the young person is an adult (whatever his age), who has earned his adulthood and hence is able to consent to contracts, or else he is still a child, and is able to work on a voluntary basis through the intermediation of parental consent.

INDEX